Early American Houses
— *with* —
A Glossary of
Colonial Architectural Terms

Norman Morrison Isham

Illustrated

DOVER PUBLICATIONS, INC.
Mineola, New York

Bibliographical Note

This Dover edition, first published in 2007, is an unabridged republication of two volumes bound as one, originally published separately by The Walpole Society, Boston, 1928 and 1939, respectively. The only significant alteration consists in making the page numbering continuous for the two separate works.

International Standard Book Number:

ISBN-13: 978-0-486-46035-2
ISBN-10: 0-486-46035-5

Manufactured in the United States of America
Dover Publications, Inc., 31 East 2nd Street, Mineola, N.Y. 11501

THE WALPOLE SOCIETY

PREFACE

THE WALPOLE SOCIETY, which holds all the arts of Early America within its view, has had the custom of publishing, from time to time, authentic texts or utterances upon those arts. The Society, in what it has already printed, has surveyed the fields of Furniture, of Ceramics and of Silver. In this book it traverses that of Architecture and examines the houses of the American Colonies in the seventeenth century.

The facts here set forth have been gathered in years of study of actual examples. The drawings and photographs presented may be relied on even where the reader may choose to disagree with theoretical statements. Of these there are not many, for the main purpose of the book has been to set out clearly the actual form of the house as it developed in plan and construction as well as in exterior and interior treatment, during the seventeenth century, along the whole Atlantic coast.

The examples have been purposely chosen, as far as has been possible, from houses not hitherto published or, at least, not well known, and, where noted houses are used, it will be found that the features presented are, in most cases, far from familiar.

CONTENTS

EARLY AMERICAN HOUSES

A GLOSSARY OF COLONIAL ARCHITECTURAL TERMS

EARLY AMERICAN
HOUSES

EARLY AMERICAN HOUSES

THE seventeenth century is the mediaeval period in American architecture. Its work is Tudor or late Gothic in character and, simple and rude as it may seem to be, has yet something of the beauty and charm with which Gothic attracts us.

It was the native tradition, English or Dutch, which our early craftsmen brought hither. They could not do otherwise. Plan, elevation and framing; windows, doors and interior finish; all were what they had used in the old home. They simply transplanted them. But while this traditional art, which had been little touched by the Renaissance, still lived on in Europe after our fathers migrated, it was, here in America, cut off from the old stem and grew in its own way and while it never lost its likeness to the European stock, it produced something, both in methods and results, which belonged to itself.

I

THE growth of the plan is quite easy to follow — early, middle, and late — beginning with the first settlements and ending about the time of the Treaty of Utrecht in 1714. In studying it we find that, in this century, we must, perforce, study the construction along with the plan and that we cannot take the framework for granted, as we can in the eighteenth century where it is almost entirely concealed. In Figures 1, 2, and 3 are shown the types of plan and the ways in which they developed. Houses seem, in the beginning, to be of the one-room or of the two-room type. In many cases the two-room type was made by putting together two single-room houses with a common roof over both and a chimney between, or else

[3]

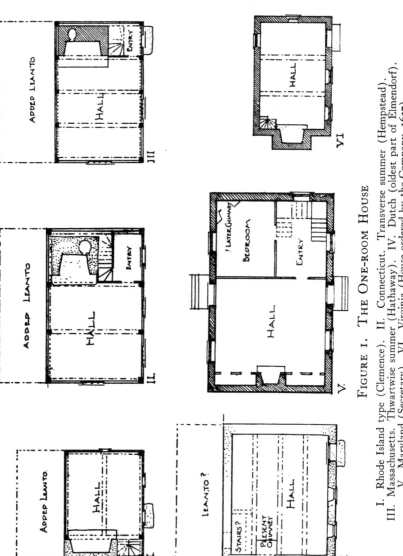

FIGURE I. THE ONE-ROOM HOUSE

I. Rhode Island type (Clemence). II. Connecticut. Transverse summer (Hempstead).
III. Massachusetts. Thwartwise summer (Hathaway). IV. Dutch (oldest part of Elmendorf).
V. Maryland (Secretary). VI. Virginia (House ordered by the Company, 1637)

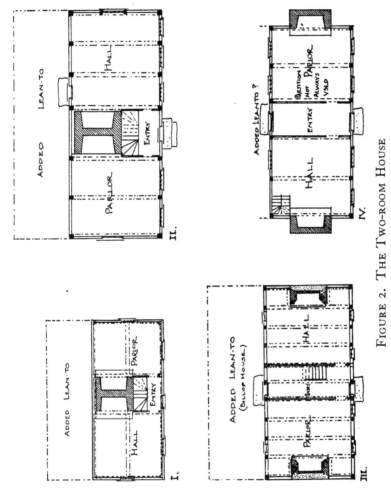

FIGURE 2. THE TWO-ROOM HOUSE

I. New England. Lengthwise summer (Fairbanks House). II. New England. Thwartwise
summer (Corwin House). III. Dutch (Schenck House). IV. Virginia

by putting together two such houses each with its end chimney. It seems, therefore, as if the original unit were a single room with a roof and a chimney. In Figure 1 is the single-room type with the end chimney. In Figure 2 (I and II) is the two-room type with the central chimney which is in general the house of New England, while in III and IV is the two-room type with end chimneys which is in general characteristic of the Middle Colonies and of the South. The type of Figure 1, the one-room house, which existed in all the colonies, was the unit.

These are, to speak generally, the early forms of the plan. The house was only one room deep. As more space was needed, rooms were added at the back and these, in New England, were covered with a leanto which, in most cases, was an addition to the original dwelling, though leantos were built as part of the house, quite early, even if they were narrow and thus of small importance. These added leantos are shown in both the figures. The next step was to put deliberately, from the start, quite important rooms, the kitchen especially, at the back. This was a fashion which was general, as the buildings and the inventories show, from about 1675. In this case the leanto, in New England, was built as a part of the house and was what we may call an original leanto. In the South, the house had, usually, simply a wider roof. The house is now two rooms deep as is shown in Figure 3.

In the next step, which was not general in New England till 1700, but occurs in Boston, in the Sargent house, as early as 1677, the plan is the same, but the back wall of the house is made of the same height as that on the front, and we have what they called, in New England at least, an "upright house."

This description is that of the seventeenth-century plan and its development as the existing houses and the documents present them to us. It must be remembered that our houses descend from the yeoman's dwelling. Any larger houses with more elaborate plans—and while almost none have come down to us

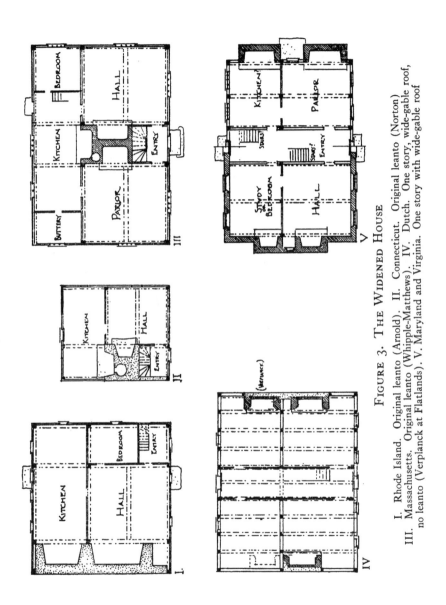

FIGURE 3. THE WIDENED HOUSE

I. Rhode Island. Original leanto (Arnold). II. Connecticut. Original leanto (Norton)
III. Massachusetts. Original leanto (Whipple-Matthews). IV. Dutch. One story, wide-gable roof,
no leanto (Verplanck at Flatlands). V. Maryland and Virginia. One story with wide-gable roof

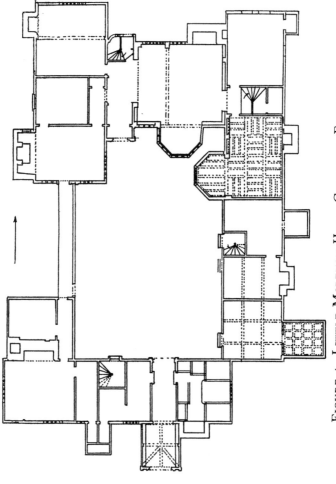

FIGURE 4. LITTLE MORETON HALL, CHESHIRE, ENGLAND

Redrawn from Garner and Stratton, *Domestic Architecture of the Tudor Period*

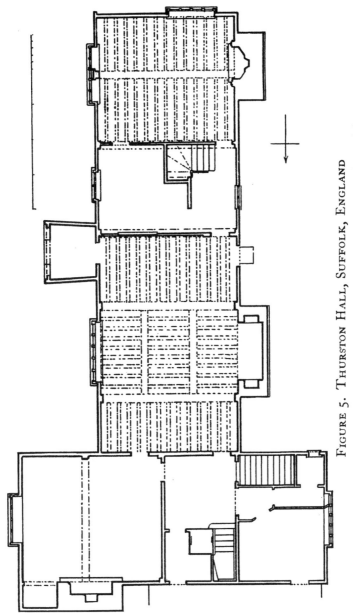

FIGURE 5. THURSTON HALL, SUFFOLK, ENGLAND

Redrawn from Garner and Stratton, *Domestic Architecture of the Tudor Period*

there must have been many which have been destroyed—could probably be accounted for by the process of putting together the single-room units. That this was often the case in England as may be seen in the plan of Little Moreton Hall, Cheshire (Figure 4), and in that of Thurston Hall, Suffolk (Figure 5). In the former, one room follows another around a courtyard. The chimneys, save in the kitchen, are on the outside. In the

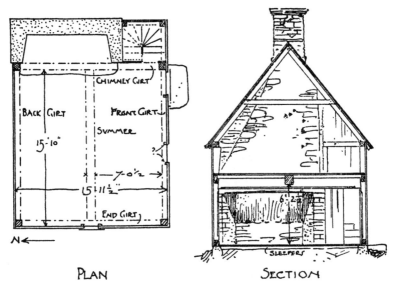

PLAN   SECTION

FIGURE 6. THE ROGER MOWRY HOUSE, PROVIDENCE, R. I.

Plan and cross section

latter, the single-room unit seems to predominate also, but the entry, with its stairs, between two rooms, gives the plan a greater likeness to our own.

We may pass over the temporary abodes of the colonists and come at once to the house with one room and, of course, an end chimney. This underwent all the changes which have been described—added leanto, original leanto, "upright," with full height at the back. Even in its simplest form it attains, in the two-story examples, to no small dignity and in the expanded plan it reaches considerable size and importance. The full two-story type appears in quite elaborate fashion in the Letitia House in Philadelphia.

A one-room plan, that of the Roger Mowry house in Providence, appears in Figure 6, with a cross-section. Figure 7 gives the plan and section of the Hathaway house in Salem in the Massachusetts Bay.

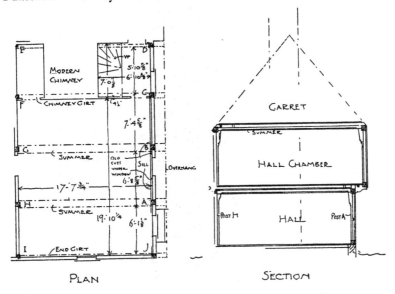

FIGURE 7. THE HATHAWAY HOUSE, SALEM, MASS.
Plan and section before restoration

The Mowry house has a post in each corner of its rather small room, at one end of which is a wide stone chimney with an enormous fireplace. This chimney does not stand on the axis of the room but leaves, on the right, as one faces it, a space in which was placed the stair or ladder to the chamber. On the left, the chimney extends to the wall of the room where, in the corner, a post is set against it. This post is part of the outside wall which thus covers the side of the chimney. On the outside of the end of the house the stack is visible for its whole width and height. In fact, it forms the greater part of the end wall, as in the Nathaniel Jenks house (Plate I).

Across the room, in front of the chimney, runs a beam called the chimney girt. In the opposite end wall of the house is one called the end girt. Between these runs a beam known among the older people as the "summer-tree," generally contracted to summer. It will be noted that in this house it runs parallel to

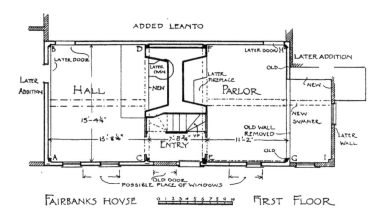

FIGURE 8. THE FAIRBANKS HOUSE, DEDHAM, MASS.

the front wall and perpendicular to the chimney. Between the corner posts run also the front girt and the back girt, and from these to the summer, across the house, run the smaller sticks called the floor joists.

The Mowry house has only a half-story in the chamber, as the second story was always called, with the plate or beam, which carries the rafters, about 3½ feet from the floor. The Southern houses which have come down to us are also a story-and-a-half in height, like the Thoroughgood house (Plate 3). In the Hathaway house the "Old Bakery," we have two full stories with a garret above (Figure 7 and Plate 2). If we examine the plan in Figure 7 we at once see some further differences. First, the chimney—the present stack is not original—did not appear on the outside. There is a girt behind the chimney and the end wall is of the usual wood construction. Then, the most important point, the summers, there are two in the room, run parallel not with the front wall but with the end wall. It is thus perpendicular not to the chimney but to the front of the house. The Narbonne house, also in Salem, has the same scheme, with but one summer, and so has the Paul Revere in Boston, and this house again has two summers. It will be seen also that each of these summers rests upon a post, as is the case in the Hempstead house in New London (II of Figure 1), and this is the usual construction. This thwartwise summer is most common in Salem and its neighborhood, but it is not universal even there, and occurs here and there in the rest of New England according to no settled rule. In the Dutch colonies and in the South, however, it seems to have been the prevailing system. Bacon's Castle has two summers which cross each other, as in some New England houses, but the thwartwise stick carries the weight.

The chimney not only showed in the outer wall of most Southern houses but projected from it as in the Thoroughgood house (Plate 3), Bacon's Castle, and others. That this was just as well known in the North is shown by the Whitfield house (Plate 4), the Pierce-Little house (Plate 5), and the Sargent, better known as the Old Province House, in Boston.

The greater number of the earlier New England houses, which have come down to us, have two rooms with a central chimney. This is the type, whether the house was built all at one time or was made up of two houses put together. The houses in Virginia are generally of the two-room type with end chimneys and sometimes, perhaps commonly, with a central entry, a hallway going across the house. It is hard to speak definitely of the New Netherlands, but documents and survivals point toward the Virginia type with the central entry.

[13]

In Figure 8 is given the plan and in Plate 6 the exterior of the Fairbanks house in Dedham, the oldest wooden house we have, built in 1637 or 1638. This house—the plan shows the original building—has but two rooms on each floor. Between them stands the chimney with the entry and stair in front of it. The eastern room, the parlor, gives no idea of its original con-

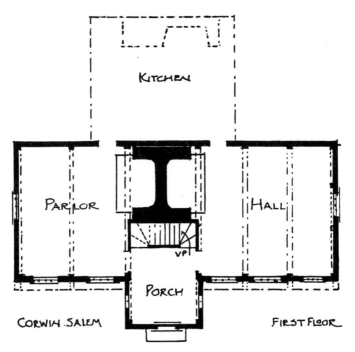

FIGURE 9. THE CORWIN HOUSE, SALEM, MASS., PLAN
1650-1675

dition. The plaster is modern. The summer is new and has been made longer than the original beam to provide for a lengthening of the room which can be seen below the gable on the outside. The hall, the western room, is far older in appearance. The horizontal sheathing on the walls, put on like clapboards, with beaded edges, may possibly be original. The old fireplace has been bricked up and the way in which the chimney girt

[14]

rests on the mantel-tree—the beam directly above the fireplace opening—is very unusual. The joists are chamfered. The sill originally projected into the room. A portion of it has been cut away for a door on the west and nearly all of it has been removed for the two doors in the entry, that now in use and the original which was a little west of this. The stairs are not old.

In the second story the parlor chamber is plastered with lime

FIGURE 10. THE CORWIN HOUSE
Original appearance

and looks quite modern. It has been lengthened, as the end girt, still in place, will show. The hall chamber is now lined with plain boards, horizontal except on the chimney wall, where they are vertical, and there still remain two moulded boards which are old. In the end wall, on the west, under the later boards, there still remains, between the heavy studs, the old clay filling on vertical sticks, one of the most important architectural fragments in America.

That there was once a stair to the garret seems probable from the care lavished upon the framing and from the large windows, remnants of which still exist in the gables. The roof, which is very steep, has no ridge and but one line of purlins on each

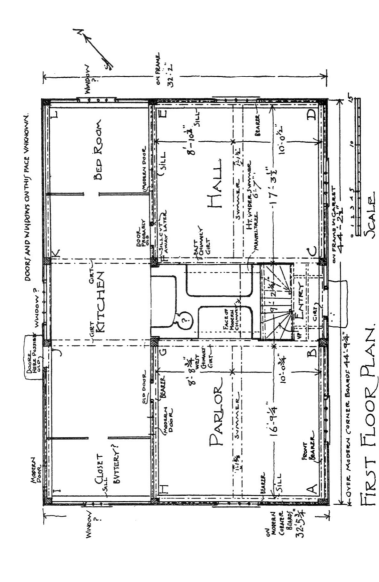

First Floor Plan.

Figure 11. Whipple-Matthews House, Hamilton, Mass.

An original leanto house

side. There is a truss over each of the chimney girts and one over each of the summers which, in the chambers, run across the house, a common device for giving a tie beam to the rafters.

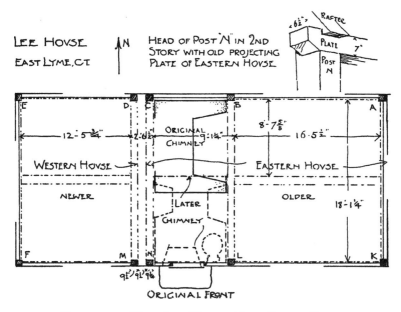

FIGURE 12. THE LEE HOUSE, EAST LYME, CONN.

Plan showing the two houses

The common rafters which are set flatwise, rest on the purlins (Figures 18 and 19), which are wind-braced to the principal rafters. It will be noted that the framing in this house is of the usual type with the lengthwise summer in the first story. The summer across the house in the second story is common, as has been said, in all houses as a tie for the truss above it.

As an example of the house of the two-room type, with the thwartwise summers, let us look at the plan in Figure 9 of the Corwin house—the so-called "Witch House"—on Essex Street, in Salem. It was probably built before 1661, as there was a "cottage right," described as "Mr. Williams'," attached to the land.

As the house now stands it has a room on the east, the old hall, with two summers crossing it and framing into posts in the front and back walls; and, on the west of the wide entry or porch, the old parlor with one summer crossing it in the same manner. On the north of these two rooms are others which

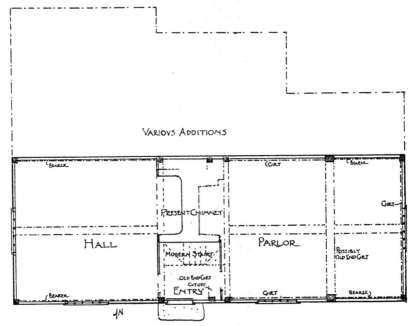

FIGURE 13. THE WHIPPLE HOUSE, IPSWICH, MASS.
End of the western or older house, after restoration

seem to be later, and the whole dwelling is now covered by a wide gambrel roof said to date from 1746. The lower slope of this, on the front, gives the pitch of the original roof.

In an old painting of the house (Plate 7) there is shown a porch, traces of which also appear in a photograph of the outside taken about 1856 (Plate 9), and are still to be seen in the house. According to the old painting this porch had a gable roof and a gable is shown on each side of it on the front of the house.

Jonathan Corwin, who bought the house in 1675, proceeded

to make some changes, and the plan in Figure 9 shows the house, presumably, as he left it. His contract with Daniel Andrews for the mason work is still extant and reads: "The said parcel of worke is to be bestowed in filling plastering and finishing a certain dwelling house bought by the said Owner," so that

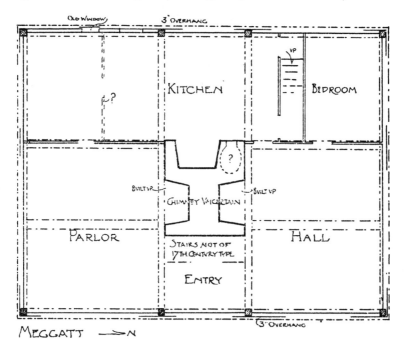

FIGURE 14. THE MEGGATT HOUSE, WETHERSFIELD, CONN.

it is not possible to claim that the house to be finished was entirely new.

An interpretation of the old painting is given in Figure 10, and in Plate 8 is an old drawing by William Twopenny, of a house in Kent, which shows very plainly the tradition which our old carpenters were following.

Somewhere about 1675—the date would vary in different places—the leanto was widened and built as a part of the house and no longer as a later addition. This, of course, does not mean that leantos were not still constantly added to old one-room or two-room houses, but that when a new house was built it was generally built with the plan two rooms deep and that the leanto was incorporated in the frame. This is shown, for the one-room house, in the Arnold and the Norton houses (I

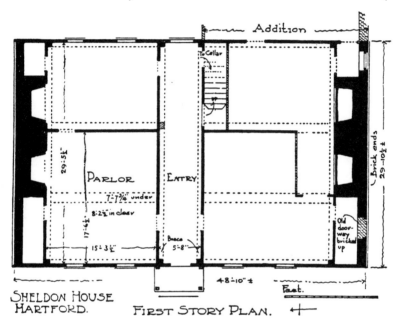

FIGURE 15. THE SHELDON HOUSE, HARTFORD, CONN.
From Isham and Brown, *Early Connecticut Houses*

and II, respectively, in Figure 3). The old hall still exists on the front and there is a kitchen on the back in the leanto with a "leanto chamber" over it. In the two-room, central-chimney houses, as in the Whipple-Matthews at Hamilton, Mass. (Figure 11), the old hall and parlor are still in the same place, while there are now three rooms, kitchen, bedroom, and buttery or kitchen and two bedrooms, at the back. The outside appearance of this type is given by Plates 11, 12 and 13.

It must not be supposed that the old house, either one-room

or two-room, without the back rooms had died out. It survived, but it is no longer characteristic. The persistence of both this and the leanto may perhaps be illustrated by the two houses, each made up of two single-room units, which appear in Figures 12 and 13, and which seem in date to belong in this period. These are the Lee house in East Lyme, and the Whipple house in Ipswich. Each house is made up of an old one-room building to which is added another single-room structure—not as an addition spliced to the frame of the older part, but as a separate frame apparently set against the former house. At the back of this combination, in each of these houses, was built a leanto addition also. This doubling of the one-room house occurs in so many instances that it must have been a common practice, with or without the leanto, and justifies the theory that our ancestors regarded the single-room house as a sort of unit of construction and plan.

The next step was the upright house. The plan of this was the same as that of the leanto house which, indeed, persisted into this late period and in some parts of the country lingered even till 1750. The rear wall, however, was now carried up to the same height as the front so that all the second-story rooms were of full height. With this there occurs, in New England at least, a slight but significant change in construction shown by the Meggatt house (Figure 14) and the Sheldon house (Figure 15). This was the leaving out of the line of posts formerly set on the back wall of the front rooms, so that the long girts spanned the whole depth of the house.

This enlargement of the house by adding rooms at the back was common in the Dutch settlements and in Maryland and Virginia as well, and we should look for the leanto there, but as almost if not quite all the seventeenth-century houses of those colonies were of one story or a story-and-a-half the leanto may not have been common. The house was widened and the roof was carried, with a slope of equal length on both sides, over the whole. Some two-story houses, however, there must have been in the South and the leanto is far too convenient a roof not to have been in some use there. There is a leanto, probably added, in the Billop house on Staten Island and Barber

CRELAWAY COVRT
(FAIRFAX HOVSE)

FIGURE 16. FAIRFAX HOUSE,
CLARK CO., VA.
Drawn from an old woodcut

in his *Historical Collections of Virginia* gives us a curious picture (Figure 16) of Lord Fairfax's house with an end chimney or end wall of stone and a long leanto roof — quite a Rhode Island "stone-ender," in fact. Of course this is not of the seventeenth century, neither is the house at Edenton, North Carolina (Plate 14), probably, but both show that the leanto was known and used in the southern colonies.

The end chimney in Rhode Island in these widened houses had two fireplaces, one for the hall and one for the kitchen, and they were usually side by side in the same stack (Plan I in Figure 3). Sometimes the second fireplace was at right angles to the first as in the Connecticut example, the Norton house (Plan II in Figure 3). In the South there are two fireplaces sometimes joined in one stack as they rise, but almost always separated above the second floor. The chimneys in those colonies were in the end walls and projected from them to a considerable distance. The Sargent house in Boston, two rooms deep, had the two fireplaces side by side with two separate projections outside in the first story. Between these there was an arch which carried the united stacks above the second floor.

While in Boston the upright house seems, if the restorations are correct, to have come in with the Sargent house before the end of the century, in the rest of New England and, with the exception of Philadelphia, probably in the Middle Colonies and perhaps in the South, the upright house appeared about 1700. Yet, the seventeenth century was not over until the old type of framing and the decoration which depended upon it had given way not merely before classic details—these can be found with the old frame and could be fastened to an old house—but before the new treatment of the plan. This took place early in some colonies, later in others. The Treaty of Utrecht, in 1714, marks quite well the coming of the colonial merchants and the great planters, the wealthy men of the world whose prosperity before the Revolution made possible the great houses of the eighteenth century.

II

THE poorer settlements and those where good stone was plentiful used that material for chimneys. Those where clay was plentiful used brick not only for chimneys but for walls. All seem to have used stone for foundations and, in stone regions like Hurley, New York, the builders used it for the whole house. There was little if any stone carving but moulded brick were used in

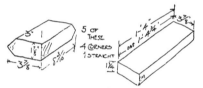

FIGURE 17. BRICK AT WHIPPLE HOUSE, IPSWICH, MASS.

chimney tops and in belts and water tables. A chimney brick is shown in Figure 17.

In New England, rocky as it is, stone houses are rare. Brick dwellings are not so scarce as those of stone, but they are not nearly so numerous as in the South.

In the wooden houses the sill, or groundsill, was laid upon the stone underpinning. The sleepers which, in the earlier houses, carried the boards of the floor were laid in the stones and the sill was placed on them. This made it project into the room. Later, especially where there was a cellar, the joists were framed into the sill.

The posts, one at each corner and one, two, or more inter-

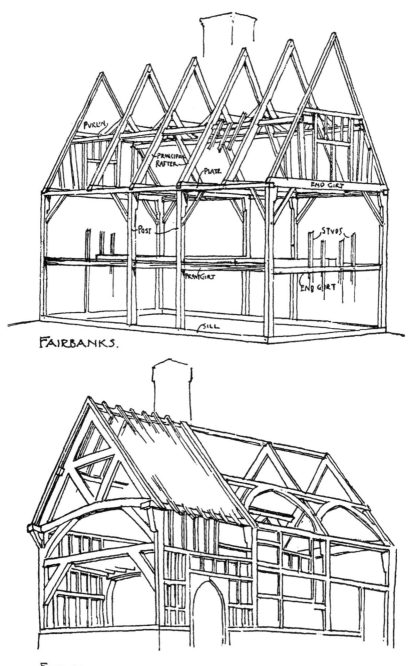

FAIRBANKS.

ENGLISH.
FROM THE STUDIO YEAR BOOK . 1921.

FIGURE 18. FRAMES. COLONIAL AND ENGLISH

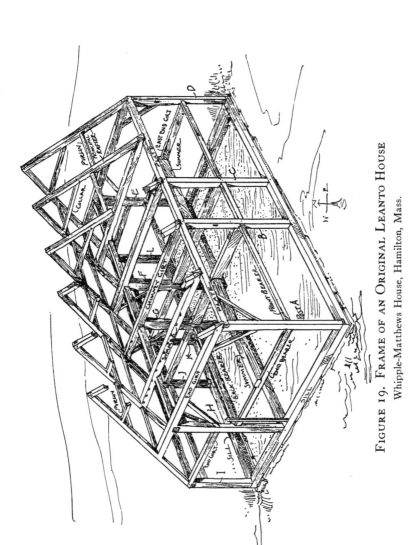

FIGURE 19. FRAME OF AN ORIGINAL LEANTO HOUSE

Whipple-Matthews House, Hamilton, Mass.

mediates on each front or end (Figures 18 and 19), stand on the sills into which they are tenoned and pinned. Between them are the girts, at the second floor level, while at their tops on the front and back are the plates or, at the ends, other girts.

Sometimes this frame was covered with vertical boarding applied to the sills, plates, and girts without any intermediate

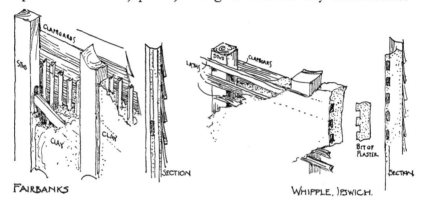

FIGURE 20. AMERICAN WATTLE AND DAUB, AND DAUB ON LATHS

framing, but in the greater number of houses the spaces between the heavier timbers are filled with lighter vertical sticks called studs and between these there were fillings, which in the earlier houses seem sometimes to have been put in before the clapboards were nailed on.

There were two common methods of wall filling in England: brick and "wattle and daub." The word "daubing," so frequent in our early documents, probably refers to the latter. The English filling consists of a mass of clay and hay plastered on both sides of a sort of basket-work, the "wattle," set between the studs. This "wattle" consisted generally of vertical rods with horizontal sticks woven between them but in East Anglia a variant[1] is found in which only the upright sticks were used[2] (Plate 15), and this appears in America. In the Fairbanks

---

[1] C. F. Innocent, *The Development of English Building Construction*, p. 129.
[2] Basil Oliver, *Old Houses and Village Buildings in East Anglia*, p. 10.

house at Dedham, Mass., the studs are quite heavy and the spaces between those in the west wall of the hall chamber are still filled with a whitish clay mixed with hay and smoothed to

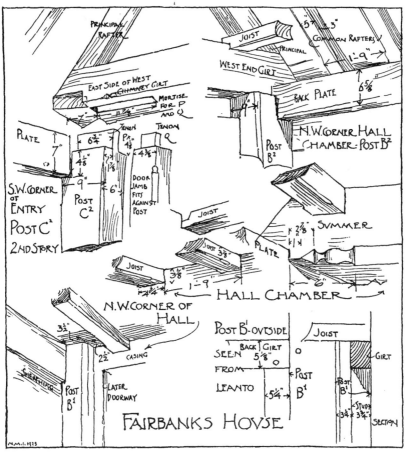

FIGURE 21. FRAMING DETAILS. FAIRBANKS HOUSE, DEDHAM, MASS.
Posts, girts, summer, joists and rafters

a fine surface. In the gable above, this same clay filling is so broken that it can be seen (Figure 20), to be plastered on both sides of upright riven sticks of oak about seven-eights of an inch thick. There is no interlacing, but a wider piece of oak is put across in front of the uprights and is sprung into grooves in the studs as is shown in the drawing. It seems, from the diary of Thomas Miner of Stonington, as if the daubing of a wall might have been done before the clapboarding and by the impression of the grain of the wood in the clay, as if the clapboard was put against the daub while it was still plastic. In the Fairbanks gable

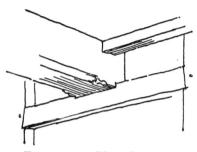

FIGURE 22. THE SUMMER.
WHIPPLE HOUSE, IPSWICH
End support in west wall of older part

one bit of daub is smooth on the outside. Another shows plainly that the clay was forced against the wood or the reverse.

In Fgure 20 there is also shown the wall filling in the Whipple house at Ipswich. Here, the studs were covered on the inside with heavy laths some distance apart and, apparently, the filling was plastered on these from the outside and then on the inside too, before the clapboards were put on, for the outer face of the fragment which was in the garret was smooth.

It should be remembered that the clapboards were originally put directly on the studs, whether over the filling or to receive it. When brick began to be used for filling, possibly because they were cheap —the daub wall is apt to be contemporary with the daub chimney — they were laid in clay in the spaces between the studs after the clapboards were put on, as they would have been disturbed by the nailing, since they were set on edge.

About 1700, and perhaps a little earlier, boards were put on the walls and to these the clapboards were nailed. These boards were horizontal and were often bevelled along their joints to keep out the weather. Shingles could be nailed to these boards, also, as they could to the vertical boards, as they evidently could not be nailed directly to the studs. In Dutch houses, with very long shingles, strips were nailed to the studs at short intervals.

The studs were generally in two lengths, one for each story, with a third for the gable, but houses occur (Figure 18) in which the studs for the two stories are all in one length, tenoned into sill and plate. In these cases the outer ends of the joists were carried on a side bearer, a stick three by six inches which ran beneath them and into which they were not framed at all.

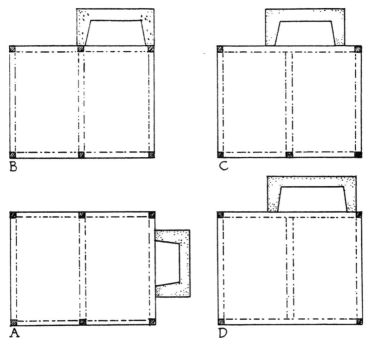

FIGURE 23. LENGTHWISE AND THWARTWISE SUMMERS

The outer end of the summer in this system was carried sometimes by an end girt and sometimes by the header over the window, as in the Whipple house (Figure 22), at Ipswich.

The summer was a heavy beam, generally of oak but sometimes of pitch pine, white pine or larch. It was 10 by 12, 12 by 12 and even larger. Its lower edge was chamfered in various ways. Along its upper edge were the mortises for the joists, which were flush with it on top. It has already been explained that it ran sometimes lengthwise of the house and sometimes thwartwise. This possibly may be explained by the suggestion that when the chimney was added to the single-room unit—which did not originally possess one— it could be added either on the side or on the end, as appears in Figure 23 at A

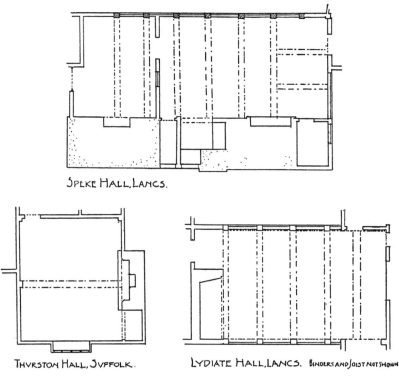

Speke Hall, Lancs.

Thurston Hall, Suffolk.   Lydiate Hall, Lancs. Binders and Joist not shown

FIGURE 24. THE SUMMER. ENGLISH PLANS

and B. The stack could not be put near the center of the end, as at C, without taking out one post, and this occurs in the Fenner house, in Cranston, R. I., and in Thurston Hall, Suffolk (Figure 24). Then the post under the outer end would go and the summer, lengthwise of the house, would frame in to the chimney girt at one end and into the end girt at the other as at D—Figure 23, which is what it almost always does in this country. When it runs across the house, however, it is almost always framed into a post. The only exceptions to this seem to be the Browne house in Watertown and one room of the Capen house in Topsfield. That this difference in the direction of the summer existed in the England of our forefathers is shown by the plans in Figure 24.

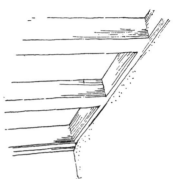

In Virginia, in the brick hous-es which are said to be the only examples left from the seven-teenth century, the summer seems to run across the house, as it does in the Tufts house and the Sargent house in New Eng-land, which are also of brick. This is true, as has been said al-ready, even of Bacon's Castle. The crosswise summer was not

FIGURE 25. THE SUMMER.
BOND'S CASTLE, MD.

Apparent arrangement. Redrawn from Sioussat, *Old Manors in the Colony of Maryland*

confined to brick houses in the South, for Mrs. Sioussat's sketch of a room in Bond's Castle, in Maryland, a wooden dwelling (Figure 25), shows heavy beams crossing the ceiling parallel with the fireplace wall. This treatment resembles that of the Dutch houses. In these there is, apparently, no special beam which can be called the summer, that is, no system of summers and joists. A series of heavy beams about four feet apart car-ries a heavy plank floor as in the houses at Hurley and in the Schenck or Crooke house (Figures 2 and 26).

Two summers crossing each other occur, as has been said, and the diagonal summer was used and still exists in one house in Ipswich.

When the summer was framed into a girt two different joints were used, one, a tusk-and-tenon, which is the older, the other, a dovetail which allowed the stick to be dropped into place. The joists also were framed into the summer or the girt in two ways: with a tusk tenon, or with a half dovetail. These are all shown in Figure 27.

When the summer is framed into a post (Plate 16), it is treated like the girt at the chimney and at the end of the house, in the second story as well as in the third, and the meeting of the various timbers on the posts brings about some very interesting framing which can be followed in the figures devoted to framing details far better than in any verbal description.

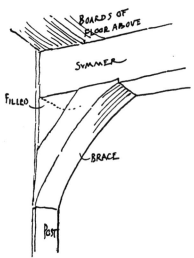

FIGURE 26. THE SUMMER. DUTCH FORM IN SCHENCK-CROOKE HOUSE, FLATLANDS, LONG ISLAND

The roof is framed sometimes with principal rafters and collar beam, purlins on which the common rafters rest, and horizontal boarding; sometimes with principal rafters, purlins, and vertical boarding. There are in this latter system no common rafters and sometimes there is no collar. These types of roof, with the details of the framing, are explained in Figure 28. The original cornice, it will be seen, was a mere eave formed by letting the rafter foot project with the boards and shingles upon it far enough to form a drip for the roof water. The later cove cornice in plaster, as it appeared in the Titcomb house, and, probably, in the Parmelee, required some special framing which is also shown in the figure. In Figure 19 is shown the framing of a roof with an original leanto.

The overhang, perhaps the most skilful bit of framing which the old carpenter produced, may be either framed or hewn. In the first form the post in the first story and that in the second are two distinct pieces of timber. In the second the upper part of a single post which runs through two stories projects beyond the lower part, and a bracket, hewn out of the post itself, marks the amount of the projection at the second floor, as in the Parmelle house, at Guilford (Figure 29). This was an ingenious device for getting rid of the

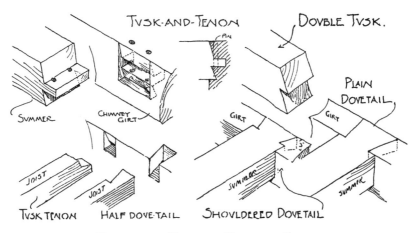

FIGURE 27. FRAMING DETAILS. JOISTS

flare or bracket at the top of the ordinary post (Figure 29) an offset used to get more room for the joints. This was gradually felt to take up too much space both for convenience and appearance on the inside of the room. The hewn overhang practically put it on the outside and left a straight post inside the house.

While the hewn overhang varies only in the shape of its bracket, there are two ways in which the framed overhang is treated; indeed, a third can be found which is a combination of these two. We might even make a fourth type, with two subdivisions, out of the manner of framing the corner where the projection was used on the ends as well as on the front or, as in the vanished "Sun Tavern," on all sides of the house.

The commonest form of the overhang is shown in Figure 29 in the Gleason house. The girt runs across the top of the post and projects beyond it anywhere from one to two feet. On the

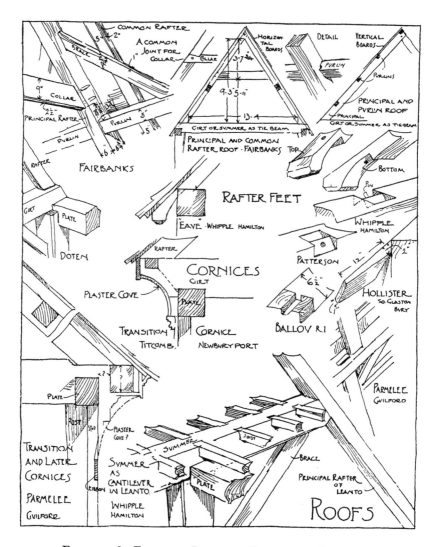

FIGURE 28. FRAMING DETAILS. ROOFS AND CORNICES

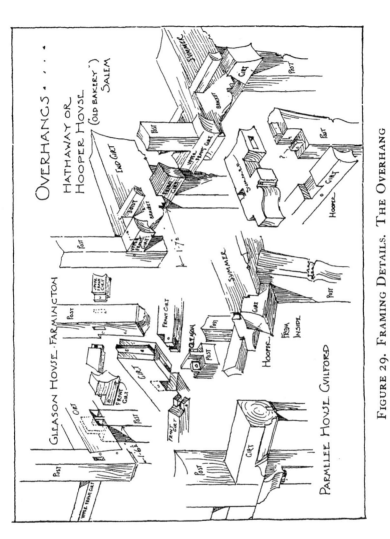

FIGURE 29. FRAMING DETAILS. THE OVERHANG

end of this girt is framed the post of the second story. The tenon is on the end of the girt and the mortise in the post which is thus allowed to continue a little distance below the under side of the girt where it ends in a more or less elaborate drop (Figures 29 and 30). A girt at the top of the first story posts takes the heads of the studs in that story and another girt, be-

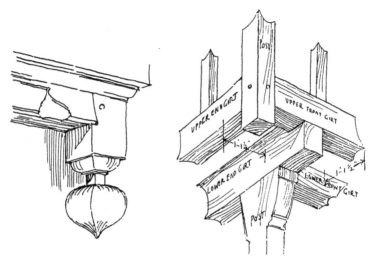

FIGURE 30. DROP OF
OVERHANG

Brown House, Hamilton, Mass.

FIGURE 32. FRAMING DETAILS.
THE OVERHANG

Corner of the Ward House, Salem, Mass.

tween the second story posts, carries the feet of the second story studding.

In the second type (Figures 31, 34, 35 and Plate 19) there is a girt at the top of the posts and studs of the first story and over this run the projecting floor joists while the girt or summer crosses the post head as in the first type. Then, on top of the ends of girt or summer and joists, is laid a sort of sill into which the second story posts and studs are framed as into the sill below. This, as will appear on a little study of the drawings, is radically different from the other system. The post stands on

OVERHANG ON FRONT

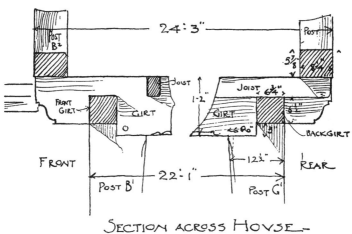

SECTION ACROSS HOUSE

FIGURE 31. FRAMING DETAILS. THE OVERHANG
Front and back wall of the Sun Tavern, Boston

the sill above the girt; it ends there; it does not run down. The girt end carries it directly and not by means of a tenon. This is the old overhang as our fathers brought it from England[1] and as it appears in the English examples in Figures 34, 35 and Plate 19.

The two systems are mixed in the Hathaway house at Salem (Figure 29). Here the posts at the ends of the house are framed upon the ends of the girts, while the intermediates stand upon the sill on the tops of the summers.

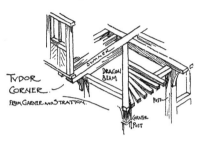

FIGURE 34. FRAMING DETAILS.
TUDOR OVERHANG

Prototype of that in the Sun Tavern, Boston

Several houses — probably, in the beginning, almost all those which had the overhang —were built with projecting ends as well as fronts, and many must originally have had the overhang on all sides, as the "Sun Tavern" and the "Old Feather Store," both in Boston, appear to have done. This called for a support for the second story post in a special way, since there was ordinarily no girt to project directly under it. There were two solutions of this problem. That in the Ward house, Salem, is given in Figure 32 from a sketch by Rev. Donald Millar. It is a combination of the two systems in that the corner post is framed upon the end of the upper front girt or sill on the tops of the girts and summers. In its turn it supports one end of the projecting upper end girt which is framed into it. The joists apparently are not used to support this end girt at all.

In the Burnham house at Ipswich, now a barn, and in the "Sun Tavern," in Boston, now destroyed, we have the other solution, the original Tudor method, the diagonal summer or

---

[1] The type used in the Gleason house occurs in the West of England.

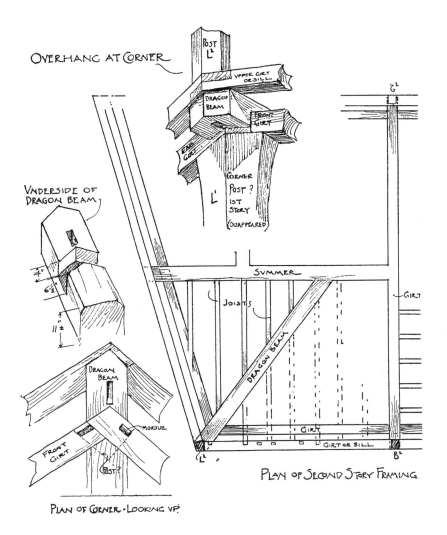

OVERHANG AT CORNER

POST L²

VPPER GIRT OR SILL

DRAGON BEAM

FRONT GIRT

END GIRT

CORNER POST? IST STORY (DISAPPEARED)

L'

VNDERSIDE OF DRAGON BEAM

4"

6'8"

11"±

DRAGON BEAM

MORTISE

FRONT GIRT

11" POST?

PLAN OF CORNER·LOOKING VP.

G²

SVMMER

JOISTS

DRAGON BEAM

GIRT

GIRT

GIRT OR SILL

L²

B²

PLAN OF SECOND STORY FRAMING.

FIGURE 33. FRAMING DETAILS. THE OVERHANG
The corner of the Sun Tavern, Boston

dragon beam. The plan of this in Figure 33 should be compared with the English prototype in Figure 34. It will be seen that the dragon extends diagonally from one of the summers

Surrey.

FIGURE 35. FRAMING DETAILS. ENGLISH FRAME WITH
OVERHANG ON FRONT
From the Studio Year Book, 1921

of the house out over the corner post in the first story (Figure 33), and carries the sill and the post in the second story exactly as the girts and summers carried their corresponding posts. Few details that have come down illustrate so well as this the close tie between the work of the Old England and that of the New.

III

Most early doors were simple affairs. Such of those on the outside as have come down to us are built up of two thicknesses of boards, the outer vertical, to shed water, the inner, horizontal. The nail heads on the outside were made a feature and arranged in more or less of a pattern. The frame of the

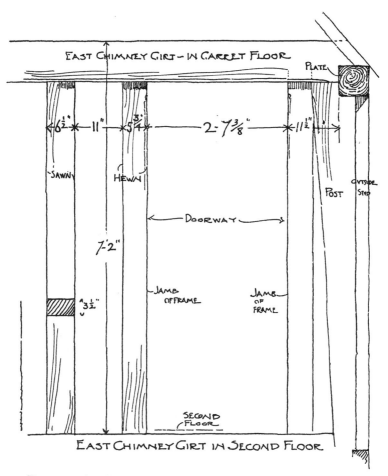

FIGURE 36. DOORS. FRAME OF DOOR FROM CHAMBER, FAIRBANKS HOUSE, DEDHAM, MASS.

outside door was part of the frame of the house. Two heavy studs were set at each side of the opening and into one or both of these, as the door was single or double, were driven the pintles to hold the hinges. The rebate seems to have been formed by the piece of wood nailed on the outside to receive the clapboards. We can judge only by the old slot cut for the wooden latch in one or two cases. In England, the head of the frame has sometimes the outline of a flat or pointed arch and,

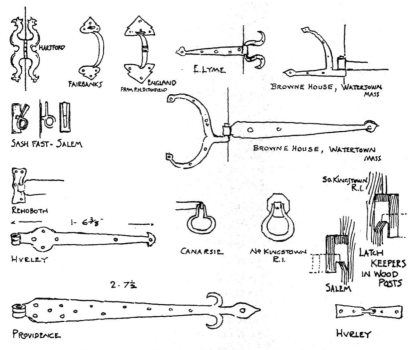

FIGURE 37. DOOR AND WINDOW HARDWARE

if we may judge by old pictures, such as the painting of the Corwin house, curved heads were in use here.

The inside doors were generally of wide, vertical sheathing with moulded edges. In fact they were part of the wall when vertical sheathing was used thereon. They were held together by battens on the back. The panelled door existed, as is shown by the example given in Plate 21, which is of real Jacobean character.

The frames of these inside doors were, in the earliest examples, as in the Fairbanks house (Figure 36), the actual studs to which they were hung with hinge and pintle. Another example, with a lighter head (Plate 20), comes from the Whipple-Matthews house, Hamilton, built in 1682.

The hardware was of iron in the better houses and followed English or Dutch tradition. The latch was managed from the outside by a drop handle which often also served as a knocker. There were locks, but none have come down to us in place. The poorer people, perhaps even the fairly well-to-do, had wooden latches with the famous latch-string. There are still wooden handles on the doors of Dean Berkeley's "Whitehall." To receive the wooden latch-bar a slot was cut in one of the jambs, as Figure 37 will show. All doors to the outside had bars. In Figure 37 are given a number of iron examples. The hinges with the circular enlargement near the pintle end are Dutch. The "cock's head" hinge, as it is called, is a very old type. It is not often found. It was used in the Jireh Bull house, Tower Hill, R. I., in 1677, and in the Sheldon-Woodbridge house at Hartford, in 1710. The hinge with the fleur-de-lys is probably 1654. The more complicated forms are from widely different places and are from inside doors. The outside doors seem to have only the heavy strap with the Dutch circle or the point or, in one example, the fleur-de-lys.

No one has ever seen, in this country, a complete seventeenth-century window in place. Old sash exist, old fragments of leaded glass without any sash appear, and a few old frames in various stages of wreck have been discovered. Out of these we have to put together a picture of the early window. In this we shall be very greatly helped by a study of the window in Tudor England, of which the window as our fathers knew it was a direct descendant, indeed, with which it was practically identical.[1] The frames, in these Tudor examples, were parts of the

---

[1] Garner and Stratton, *Domestic Architecture of England in the Tudor Period*, II, plates of wood detail.

framing of the house. The studs formed the jambs, the headers above and below were the actual head and sill. These pieces, except, perhaps, the sill, were moulded and, in the usual form of window, the mullions, as they are called, which separated the lights or openings, were moulded also (Plate 22).

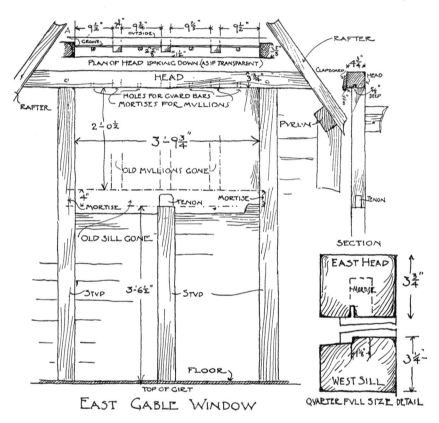

EAST GABLE WINDOW

FIGURE 38. WINDOWS. FRAME IN EAST GABLE OF FAIRBANKS HOUSE, DEDHAM, MASS.

There was very often a transom which, too, was moulded on the under side. The head sometimes projected beyond the face of the frame and the sill was often made to do likewise. Most of the glazing, which was sometimes bequeathed in wills as something separate from the house, was set into the frames without sash and was fastened to two upright pieces of wood, the guard-bars let into the head and sill on the inside. Where there were swinging casements they were apt to be of iron.

Our windows occur as single, triple, and quadruple, that is

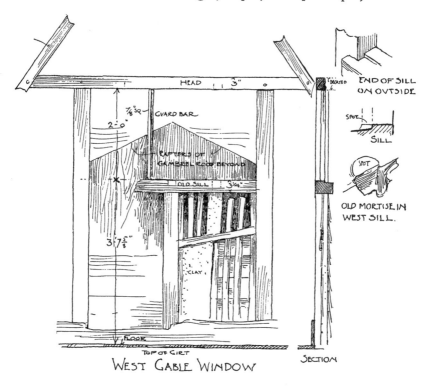

WEST GABLE WINDOW   SECTION

FIGURE 39. WINDOWS. FRAME IN WEST GABLE OF FAIRBANKS HOUSE, DEDHAM, MASS.

one- three- and four-light. Double or two-light windows must have been used, especially in brick and stone houses where the span had to be small, but none have come down.

The single windows we have are unbelievably small. In the vertically boarded house in Rhode Island and probably wherever this type of wall was used, we find two studs for the

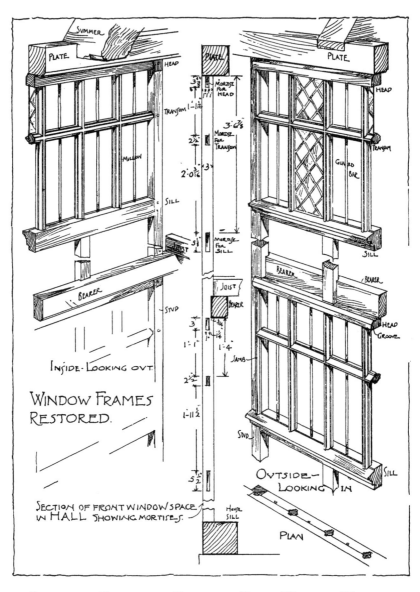

FIGURE 40. FOUR-LIGHT FRAMES IN FRONT WALL OF WHIPPLE-
MATTHEWS HOUSE, HAMILTON, MASS.

jambs of the frame. The mortises for these are still in the Arnold house, and the clear space there is only 12½ inches. In some other houses which are vertically boarded we find studs spaced at greater distances, and these mark the width of an ancient opening of several lights. No frame for such a window, in a plank house exists. In a house at Lincoln, R. I., are two

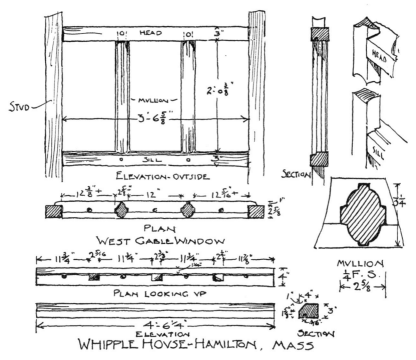

FIGURE 41. WINDOWS. OLD THREE-LIGHT FRAME IN GABLE, WHIPPLE-MATTHEWS HOUSE, HAMILTON, MASS.

studs, presumably for a single-light window, and in each, at a considerable height from the floor, is a gain cut at a very sharp bevel which may mark the ancient sill.

The oldest window frames in the colonies are those of the four-light windows in the gables of the Fairbanks house. That in the east gable (Figure 38) has lost its sill and its mullions, but the sill mortises still exist in the old studs which form the jambs, while those of the mullions are still to be seen in the ancient head which retains also the groove to receive the tops of the sheets of leaded glass. The guard-bar holes, too, are still visible. In the west window (Figure 39) the head, while it is still in place, is badly decayed on the outside, but the frame

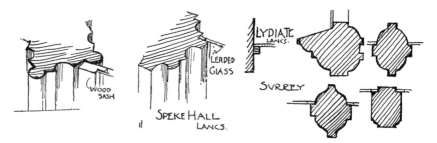

FIGURE 42. WINDOWS. ENGLISH MULLIONS, JAMB AND TRANSOM

retains over half of its ancient sill, also partly rotted away and though the mullions are gone, the mortises remain. One guard-bar, too, is still in place. Around one mortise in the sill is a curious raised place which looks almost as if it were made, as a "spot" on a stone sill would be, to receive the mullion. The whole frame is part of the frame of the house, like the old English window frame in Plate 22.

The jambs are not moulded and leave open the question of the way in which the clapboards were stopped against the edge of the opening. In Tudor times the jamb stud was adjusted to half-timber work, so that there were no clapboards. The lack of moulding also leaves open the question: how was the rebate formed to hold the glass? In this frame the glass would come against the smooth square face of the jamb. This sometimes happened in England and, in one example, at Lydiate Hall, a strip was set on the jamb to form the rebate. Generally the Tudor jamb had the same moulding as the mullion and into this the glass fitted (Figure 42), just as it would fit into the mullions of this frame. That wooden sash could be fitted to the mullion is shown in the same figure.

Traces of other ancient frames were found in the Whipple-Matthews house, Hamilton, Mass. Here there were, in both stories (Figure 40), the jamb studs for several windows with

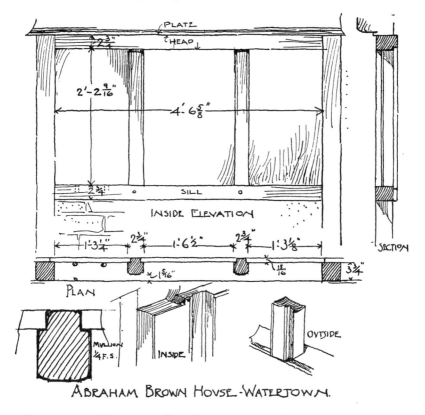

ABRAHAM BROWN HOUSE-WATERTOWN.

FIGURE 43. WINDOWS. OLD THREE-LIGHT FRAME IN ABRAHAM BROWNE HOUSE, WATERTOWN, MASS.

the mortises for the head, the transom, and the sill. There was one four-light window in each of the two outer sides of the hall and the hall chamber and, no doubt, in the other front room as well, but in the parlor the studding for the front window had been cut away and lost. Sills, transoms, and heads had been removed, but what had been used as a jack stud for a later opening turned out to be an old window head complete except that its tenons had been sawed off. On the under side of this were the mortises for the mullions and the marks which gave the entirely English profile of the mullion moulding.

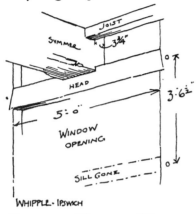

FIGURE 44. WINDOWS. WHIPPLE
HOUSE, IPSWICH
Old opening in west end of older part

In the west gable of the garret, however, there was found a triple window frame with head, sill and mullions, but with no transom and with no jambs except the bare studs at the sides and these did not belong to that frame. The head and sill had been hewn off on the front to allow the later boarding to cover them, and the whole frame had probably been set back for the same purpose.

The sill probably had a moulded edge. The head (Figure 41), can be exactly restored, in section, from the old head found in the parlor wall. How this old frame looked can be seen in the photograph (Plate 23) and in the measured drawings (Figure 41). Something had been hewn away on the bottom of this old sill also, for the two ends are not of the same depth. There were no jambs in any of these frames except the studs at the sides. This agrees with the Fairbanks house frames and may have been what Moxon meant when he said that sometimes there were no separate window jambs or posts.[1]

At the Abraham Browne house in Watertown, Mass., an early frame came to light. This, which is shown in Figure 43 and Plates 24 and 25, has sill, mullions, and head, but the jambs, again, are only the studs at the sides. Here,

---

[1] Quoted by C. F. Innocent, *op. cit.*, p. 260.

there must have been a strip on the outer face of the stud as was suggested for the Whipple house in Plate 26, to receive the clapboards and to form a rebate for the glass, for the corner of the studs aligns with the corner of the rebate in

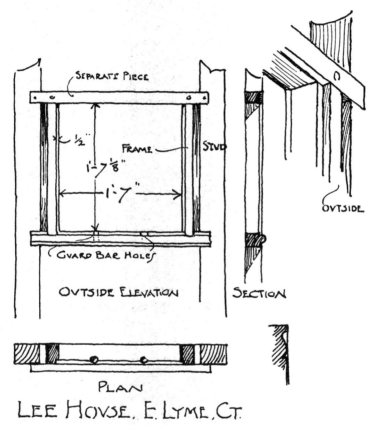

LEE HOVSE, E. LYME, CT.

FIGURE 45. WINDOWS. OLD FRAME IN LEE HOUSE

the mullion, which has no longer the older English moulded form.[1] The back of the sill is flush with the inside face of the stud. The middle opening in this window has a wooden sash, as the pintles had left plain traces. Indeed, a fragment of one

---

[1] See the lower right hand of Figure 42.

was in place. A restoration of this window is used in the seventeenth-century room of the American Wing.

In figure 44 is the frame of a window in the west wall of the Whipple house at Ipswich, which has head and jambs but no sill, though the pin for the latter is to be seen in one of the jambs.

In the Lee house at East Lyme, Conn. (Figure 45 and Plate 26), there is a frame for a single light. Here the head and sill are gained into the studs but the latter do not form the jambs. These are rebated pieces of oak framed into the head and sill a little way inside the face of the studs. The outer edge of the sill projects in a half-round above a flat surface meant to be covered by the clapboards. On the inner edge of each jamb there is an old moulding. The head and sill are plain on the inside and all the corners are square. There are no hinge marks and no sash, but the holes for the guard-bars are there and so is the groove in the head to take the glass.

In the jambs of the Lee house frame and in the mullions of that in the Browne house there were square rebates in which sash could shut, but there was a sash only in the middle light of the Browne house window. In the other two openings of that frame the glass, without any sash, was simply set in place and secured to the guard-bars by strips of lead soldered to the calmes of the glazing. There is no rebate in the head at the Lee house, nor in any of the other heads above described. There were no sash in any of them, unless possibly in the lower of the transom windows in the Whipple-Matthews house. In all of them the top of the sheet of leaded glass was put into the groove in the head of the frame and then secured to the guard-bars. The glass was stationary in the sense that it could not be swung open or shut. It had to be put in and taken out. Some sheets of leaded glass have been preserved, without sash, which seem to have been designed for this use.

The wooden sash preserved in the museums are too large to

fit the grouped windows at the Fairbanks and Whipple houses or even the single frame at the Lee house. The middle light in the Browne house, alone, is large enough to take such a sash, as we know it did.

A contract in 1657 says: "the two windows are to be two foote lights of foote broad and a foote and onehalf long." These seem to have been in the garret. In the chambers for each window: "three lights of two foote long and one foot broad; the lower rooms, the two windows are to be four lights, two feet in length."[1] These are practically the sizes in the Whipple house. The lights in the Fairbanks house are even narrower, though of the same length. The wooden sash of William Coddington's house is 1'-7½" by 2'-3⅜", a size which, when we subtract from it the stiles and rails, gives us glass very nearly 1'-4" by 2'-0". A sash in Plymouth is 16¾" by 22½", which gives a width of 1'-1" for the glass. In the Essex Institute is one 1'-8¼" by 2'-4⅝", which leaves 1'-4¾" for width of glass. This sash still has its hinges, one at each corner, and the old fast or turnbuckle on the opposite stile. There is another at Hartford, 1'-4¹⁄₁₆" wide and 2'-6⅝" high. It has a transom. It looks as if it had, at first, been used in a narrow opening and as if it had, later, been set with another in a wider space, since an astragal has been put on one stile. The marks of the hinges are still to be seen on the wood.

In the Coddington sash, one at Deerfield, one in Boston, and one in Salem, the glass is in rectangular panes. The others have diamond-shaped quarrels.

---

[1] Eben Putnam.

IV

THE treatment of the interior of the house depended very closely on the construction. This was, in early work especially, almost entirely apparent; and in the houses of the poorer people it remained so to an almost painful extent, and made them bare and forbidding. In the better homes, however, the treatment of the rooms left little to be desired and the artistic value, in both form and color, reached a very high point.

The ceilings consisted of the summers and joists of the floor above, or, in the Dutch houses, of the summers and the planking. The girts in the corners between the walls and the floor above took the place of the cornice, even if, as in the Dutch colonies, there was little projection. In New England, the summers and girts were chamfered. This is so strict a rule that we may doubt the age of any unchamfered heavy beam. Among the Dutch the bead is often used. The chamfer occurs but it is rarely met. The joists were sometimes chamfered also, but by no means always. The spaces between them were sometimes plastered, as in the "Sun Tavern," but usually the underside of the floor boards above formed the real surface of the ceiling. This was allowed to color at its own will, and with sunlight and wood smoke it generally darkened beautifully. In some rooms, as years went on, it darkened too much and then whitewash was applied to it. Some of these old ceilings, especially those with several summers or with summers that crossed each other, or those like the "Sun Tavern," with summer and dragon beams, were splendid productions. The mediaeval quality of our old work is nowhere more clearly to be seen.

There were four ways of treating the walls of a seventeenth-century room: plaster between the studs, plaster over the studs, vertical boarding, and horizontal boarding.

CLAY BETWEEN STYDS

FIGURE 46. INTERIORS. PLASTER OR CLAY FILLING
BETWEEN STUDS

It is curious that, as a general rule, whatever the treatment of the other walls of the room may be, the fireplace end, in the houses as we have them, is vertically boarded.

The earliest wall treatment we have is that in the hall chamber and in the garret of the Fairbanks house. Its construction

CLAY OVER STVDS

FIGURE 47. INTERIORS. PLASTER OF CLAY OR LIME
OVER STUDS

(Figure 20) has already been explained. Its general appearance is given in Figure 46, while the English prototype is shown by Plate 27. In this English example there are fragments of paneling on the wall, a proof that this construction was not always left bare as it certainly was in other instances. The paneling may be later than the frame, as is the present horizontal boarding in the Fairbanks house. The known practice in

England, with the constant allusions to daubing in our early records, makes it very certain that this type of interior represents a controlling manner for the earlier days of the colonies. It certainly made a picturesque interior.

This chimney end of the room is now vertically boarded and

FIGURE 48. INTERIORS. HORIZONTAL BOARDING OR WAINSCOT

some of the boards are old and show that it was so boarded a long time ago. But the heavy stud of the entry door-jamb toward the chimney and the one next to it seem to indicate that there may have been, originally, a wattle and daub partition even here.

Plaster between the studs was, apparently, not only English but Dutch, for we find it, with the character of the filling unknown but probably of clay backed against the laths or strips for the outside shingles, in the Crooke-Schenck house at Flatlands, Long Island (Plate 28). The final coats were apparently of lime and not of clay.

Plastering over the studs (Figure 47) was done in two ways: on laths nailed to the inside faces of the studs, or on a filling of

FIGURE 49. INTERIORS. ROOM FROM CROWHURST PLACE, SURREY, ENGLAND

Vertical "post and pane." The beginning of vertical sheathing.
Redrawn from Gotch, *The Growth of the English House*

brick which probably soon began to take the place of the wattle and daub between the timbers.

The Whipple house at Ipswich, while it has been restored, still gives, in its hall chamber (Plate 29), an excellent example of the effect of plastering on laths as the seventeenth century knew it. The construction of the wall, which is shown in Figure 20, can be examined in the glazed panel beyond the post on the right-hand wall (Plate 30).

This room has vertical boarding on the fireplace end as does the Hart house parlor (Plate 31), another good example, also from Ipswich, of a room plastered on three sides. This can be studied in the reproduction of it now in the American Wing at the Metropolitan Museum of Art.

FIGURE 50. INTERIORS. VERTICAL BOARDING OR WAINSCOT

The chamber in the Abraham Browne house was plastered on three walls and vertically boarded on the chimney end. In Plate 24 the brick filling of the wall is plainly shown. Over this filling the plaster was spread and a skim was carried over the studs and braces, the faces of which were hacked, as the figure shows, to provide a clinch for it.

The walls of rooms were boarded horizontally (Figure 48) very early, whatever filling was used, for the sake of the added warmth if not for the appearance. The first mention of this "wainscot" occurs in Governor Winthrop's famous rebuke to

Mr. Ludlow, whose reply: "it was for the warmth of his house
. . . being but clapboards nailed to the wall in the form of
wainscott," fixes the name and the practice.

The hall in the Fairbanks house (Plate 32) is boarded horizontally in this clapboard fashion with a bead on the bottom of
each board and this may be very old. In most of the horizontal
wainscot, however—and very many rooms have it—the boards
are not lapped, but are tongued-and-grooved together with
mouldings at the joints. The American Wing has an excellent
example (Plate 33) in the hall of the Capen house. Even here, it
will be noted, the fireplace end of the room is boarded vertically.

The beginning of our vertical boarding or wainscot is to be
seen in the room at Crowhurst Place, Surrey (Figure 49).
There we have a series of heavy uprights—some of them, at any
rate, practically studs—with thin pieces between them ploughed,
like panels, into each. Our work is, like the horizontal sheathing, of a series of light boards (Figure 50) of equal thickness,
grooved together, with mouldings at the joints. Generally
these boards are set continuously, that is, one board exactly re-
peats another, except in width, but once in a while there is an
echo of the Crowhurst arrangement—a board with both edges
moulded alike, into which that on each side is fitted.

At first, the vertical boarding appears on the fireplace end of
the room, and, as has been said, was used there, as in the Hart
and Capen house rooms, whatever the treatment of the other
walls. It appears very early in the Doten house at Plymouth,
as the actual outside covering of a vertically boarded house.
Later, it was used for all the walls of the room in the stud-
wall houses, as in the Lee house at East Lyme, Conn.

This fashion, because, probably, of its use on the fireplace
wall, lingered quite late. There are, in one house in Norwich,
three rooms with vertical boarding. They vary in their fireplace ends. One has vertical boarding, the second has the ver-

tical boarding with a panel over the fireplace opening and the third has paneling over that whole end.

Old stairs are hard to find. Here and there, in a cellar flight, appears the mediaeval type in which solid steps made by sawing a beam on its diagonal were pinned to joists or "stayers," but no instance of this has survived in the first story, if it ever existed. In the one-room houses, the stairs in the corner next the chimney were probably of the mediaeval corkscrew type, all winders. There were traces of such a flight in the Abraham Browne house. The stairs in the central-entry houses were probably at first all partitioned off, that is, on the side toward the entry there was, except where the stair began, a straight piece of partition. We are well along toward the eighteenth century, if not actually in it, before we find an open rail or a rail with balusters.

If the test of any period of domestic architecture lies in its interiors our old houses should rank well. They fitted the life of their time as this life made them and fitted them. For the interior in those days was not produced by the whim of an owner or the mood of an artist. It was an actual correspondence of a state of mind and a manner of life.

If these pages have succeeded in giving the true picture they have tried to draw of the house of the seventeenth-century American they have shown that the work in it was like that in Europe and yet unlike it, and that it was good; that our fathers began to be Americans at the very foundation of the colonies and that they prized at once their independence and their art; so that we can really speak, and speak with pride, of American seventeenth-century architecture.

EARLY AMERICAN
HOUSES
─────────

PLATES

PLATE I. THE JENKS HOUSE, PAWTUCKET, RHODE ISLAND

Outside chimney on west end now destroyed

PLATE 2. THE HATHAWAY HOUSE ("OLD BAKERY"), SALEM, MASS.

Built in 1685. From a photograph showing it on its original site

PLATE 3. THE ADAM THOROUGHGOOD HOUSE,
PRINCESS ANNE COUNTY, VIRGINIA

Showing chimney projecting from the outer wall in the southern manner

PLATE 4. THE WHITFIELD HOUSE, GUILFORD, CONN.

PLATE 5. PIERCE-LITTLE HOUSE, NEWBURY, MASS.

House said to have been built in 1651. This shows outside chimney
at rear of present ell

PLATE 6. THE FAIRBANKS HOUSE, DEDHAM, MASSACHUSETTS

PLATE 7. THE CORWIN HOUSE, SALEM, MASS.
From a painting made about 1819

PLATE 8. THE CORWIN'S PROTOTYPE-HOUSE AT BRENCHLEY, KENT, ENGLAND

From a drawing by William Twopenny

PLATE 9. THE CORWIN HOUSE, SALEM, MASS.

From a photograph made about 1856

PLATE 10. THE WHIPPLE-MATTHEWS HOUSE,
HAMILTON, MASS.

The front with later cornice and windows

PLATE 11. THE "COBBET" HOUSE, IPSWICH, MASS.

PLATE 12. THE NORTON HOUSE, GUILFORD, CONN.

PLATE 13. WHIPPLE HOUSE, IPSWICH, MASS.
Western end showing addition of leanto

PLATE 14. HOUSE AT EDENTON, NORTH CAROLINA

PLATE 15. WATTLE AND DAUB IN ENGLAND
From Oliver. *Old Houses and Villages in East Anglia*

PLATE 16. SUMMER AND POST

Thwartwise summer on post head in Hathaway house, Salem, Mass., before restoration.
Courtesy of George Francis Dow

PLATE 17. OVERHANG, HATHAWAY HOUSE, SALEM, MASS.
Seen from below, looking west, before restoration.
Courtesy of George Francis Dow

PLATE 18. OVERHANG OF HATHAWAY HOUSE,
SALEM, MASS.

Seen from below, looking east, before restoration.
Courtesy of George Francis Dow

PLATE 19. ENGLISH HOUSE

Front and end overhang. From a drawing by W. Twopenny

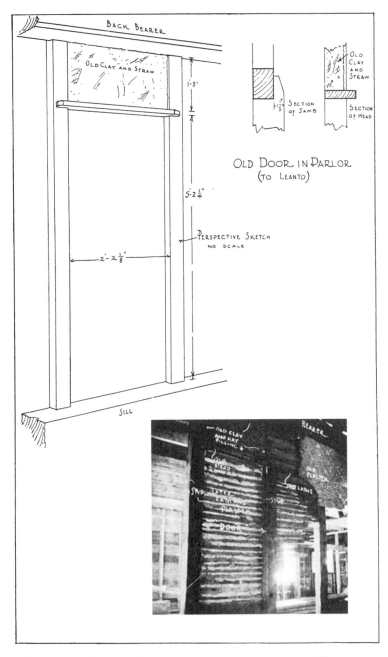

BACK BEARER

OLD CLAY AND STRAW

1'-3"

5'-2¼"

2'-2⅛"

SILL

SECTION OF JAMB

1⅜"

OLD CLAY AND STRAW

SECTION OF HEAD

OLD DOOR IN PARLOR
(TO LEANTO)

PERSPECTIVE SKETCH
NO SCALE

OLD CLAY AND HAY FILLING

BEARER

OLD PLASTER

2ND LAYER LATHING PLASTER

2ND LATHS

STUD

DOOR

PLATE 20. DOORS. FRAME OF OLD INSIDE DOOR IN WHIPPLE-
MATTHEWS HOUSE, HAMILTON, MASS.

PLATE 21. DOORS. INSIDE DOOR
WITH JACOBEAN PANELLING

PLATE 22. WINDOWS. OLD FRAME AT SALISBURY, ENGLAND

PLATE 23. WINDOWS. OLD THREE-LIGHT FRAME
IN GABLE OF WHIPPLE-MATTHEWS HOUSE,
HAMILTON, MASS.

I. From inside. II. From outside.
Photographs taken after removal

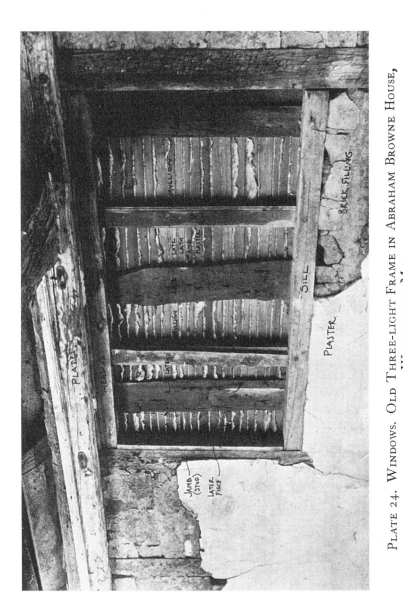

PLATE 24. WINDOWS. OLD THREE-LIGHT FRAME IN ABRAHAM BROWNE HOUSE, WATERTOWN, MASS.

View from inside.   Courtesy of Society for the Preservation of New England Antiquities

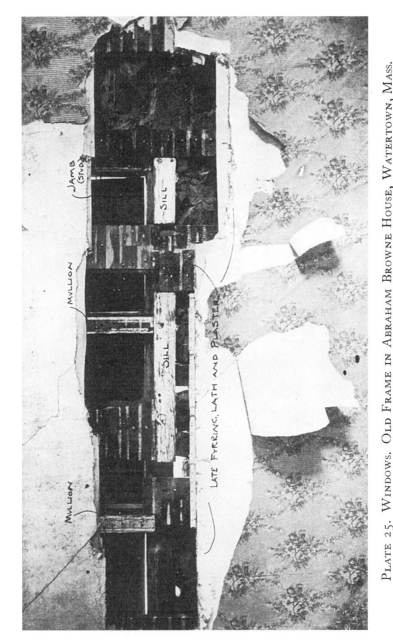

PLATE 25. WINDOWS. OLD FRAME IN ABRAHAM BROWNE HOUSE, WATERTOWN, MASS.

Courtesy of Society for the Preservation of New England Antiquities

PLATE 26. WINDOWS. OLD FRAME
IN LEE HOUSE

View from outside

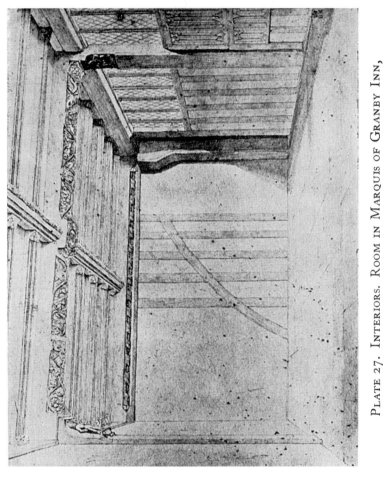

PLATE 27. INTERIORS. ROOM IN MARQUIS OF GRANBY INN, COLCHESTER, ENGLAND

Plaster between studs. From a drawing by W. Twopenny

PLATE 28. INTERIORS. SCHENCK-CROOKE HOUSE, FLATLANDS, NEW YORK

Plaster between studs.   Courtesy of Dr. G. W. Nash

PLATE 29. INTERIORS. HALL CHAMBER,
WHIPPLE HOUSE, IPSWICH

Plaster over studs; restored

PLATE 30. INTERIORS. HALL CHAMBER,
WHIPPLE HOUSE, IPSWICH

Plaster over studs; restored

PLATE 31. INTERIORS. HART HOUSE PARLOR REPRODUCED IN AMERICAN
WING AT THE METROPOLITAN MUSEUM OF ART, NEW YORK

Plaster on three walls over studs; vertical boarding on chimney end

PLATE 32. INTERIORS. HALL IN FAIRBANKS HOUSE, DEDHAM, MASS.

Horizontal sheathing over older clay-filled stud wall

PLATE 33. INTERIORS. CAPEN HOUSE HALL REPRODUCED IN AMERICAN WING AT METROPOLITAN MUSEUM OF ART, NEW YORK

Vertical sheathing on fireplace end; horizontal on side wall

INDEX

INDEX

INDEX

INDEX

INDEX

INDEX

INDEX

Pin, 26
Pine, pitch, 29
    white, 29
Pintle, 42, 43, 51
Places
    Boston, 13, 22, 37, 38, 53
    Brenchley, Eng., *pl.* 8
    Canarsie, N. Y., 42
    Cheshire, Eng., 8
    Clark Co., Va., 22
    Colchester, Eng., *pl.* 27
    Cranston, R. I., 30
    Dedham, Mass., 12, 14, 27,
        41, *pls.* 6, 32
    Deerfield, Mass., 53
    East Lyme, Conn., 17, 21,
        42, 51, 52, *pl.* 26
    Edenton, N. C., *pl.* 14
    England, *see* that word
    Flatlands, L. I., 7, 57, *pl.*
        28
    Guilford, Conn., 33, 34,
        pls. 4, 12
    Hamilton, Mass., 16, 20, 25,
        36, 43, 46, 47, *pls.* 10,
        20, 23
    Hartford, 20, 43, 53
    Hurley, N. Y., 23, 31, 42
    Ipswich, Mass., 18, 21, 28,
        29, 31, 38, 50, 52, 58,
        59, *pls.* 11, 13, 29, 30
    Lancashire, Eng., 30
    Lincoln, R. I., 47
    Long Island, 58
    Newbury, Mass., *pl.* 5
    New London, 13
    New Netherlands, 13
    North Kingstown, R. I., 42
    Pawtucket, R. I., *pl.* 1

Places
    Philadelphia, 11
    Plymouth, 60
    Princess Anne Co., Va., *pl.*
        3
    Providence, 10, 11, 42
    Rehoboth, Mass., 42
    Salem, 11, 13, 14, 17, 53
    Salisbury, Eng., *pl.* 22
    South Kingstown, R. I., 42
    Staten Island, 22
    Stonington, Conn., 28
    Suffolk, Eng., 9, 30
    Surrey, Eng., 48, 60
    Topsfield, Mass., 31
    Tower Hill, R. I., 43
    Watertown, Mass., 31, 42,
        49, 50, *pls.* 24, 25
    Wethersfield, Conn., 19
Plan, growth of, 3
    new treatment of, 23
    types of, 3
        one-room, 3, 4, 6, 11, 20
        two-room, 5, 17, 20
        two-rooms deep, 20
Plank, 31, 54
Plaster, 14, 15, 19, 28, 34, 54, 55,
    56, 59, *pls.* 29, 30, 31
Plate, 12, 25, 26, 29, 34
Post, 21, 27, 30, 32, 34, *pls.* 16,
    27, 30
    corner, 23, 39
    intermediate, 23, 24, 25
    overhang, in, 32, 35, 37, 38,
        39
    see other framing drawings
Purlin, 15, 17, 25, 32, 34
Putnam, Eben, 53

INDEX

INDEX

A GLOSSARY
OF
COLONIAL ARCHITECTURAL
TERMS
with Author's Illustrations

THE WALPOLE SOCIETY

PREFACE

*T*HE *old architects or housewrights as well as the masons, the carpenters and the "joyners," had a language of their own. Their successors have a good deal of it still, but they have lost many words and have, with the progress of the world, acquired possibly even more new ones.*

The antiquary, the interested visitor to the museum or to our old houses and even the architect are sometimes at a loss for the meaning of these old words—the new do not often intrude. The question, "what is a summer?" is not unheard in Early American Rooms.

The Walpole Society, in following its declared purpose, "the pursuit, the acquisition, the enjoyment, the naming and the verification of things which may well be considered decently ancient, or charming, or beautiful—or all three," has put forth already three Glossaries for Collectors—of Furniture, of Ceramics, and of Silver. It now follows these with a Glossary for the Collector of Old Houses.

This is not a general architectural dictionary—it knows nothing of Greek or Gothic as such. It intends to gather here and to define not only such terms of design and construction as may be needed by the visitor to Colonial Rooms or to old houses perhaps well known, perhaps by the wayside, but those curious words as well which are used in old contracts and in the old records whether of State, Church, or College, words which are not only venerable but of the greatest interest.

NORMAN MORRISON ISHAM

A GLOSSARY

OF

COLONIAL ARCHITECTURAL

TERMS

ABACUS. The crowning mem-

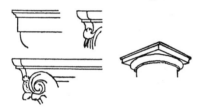

ber of a capital, *q. v.* It varies with the order used.

ANCHOR. A bar of wrought iron fastened to the end of a beam and built into a brick or stone wall, or sometimes carried through the wall and secured by a cross-iron in the shape of an S.

ARCH. An arrangement of radiating wedge-shaped stones or of

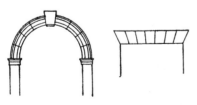

brick with wedge-shaped joints which are set in the form of a curve, a half-circle, a segment or an ellipse, or even on a level line. The stones or bricks are called voussoirs, *q. v.* The word is used for the same forms when built up of wood.

ARCH ORDER. An arch which has on the pier at either side an engaged column or a pilaster, *q. v.*,

carrying an entablature with or without a pediment. It is rare, but an analogous form is very common in wooden door frames in later work.

ARCHITRAVE. The lowest

ARCHITRAVE. (Cont'd) member of an entablature, *q. v.*, resting on the abaci of the column

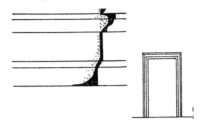

capitals. Also used of both the horizontal and the vertical stone or wood trimming or casing around a square or rectangular opening.

ARCHIVOLT. The moulding of an architrave carried around the face of an arch, *q. v.*

ASHLAR. Stone cut square so that the exposed faces are rectangles. *See* Rustication.

ASTRAGAL. A small half round moulding. It generally has a fillet on one or both sides. *See* Bead, Neck Moulding.

ATTIC. A modern word for the garret.

BACK BAND. The outer moulding of a door or window casing, *q. v.*

BALUSTER. A turned or rectangular upright supporting a stair rail. It is set between this rail and the stair step, or the floor, or the top of a closed string. *See* Stair. Used also on the outside of a building.

BALUSTRADE. The combination of posts, rail and balusters of a stair, *q. v.*, or of posts, bottom rail, top rail and balusters above a cornice on the outside of a building.

BAR. A small moulded piece of wood separating the panes of glass in a sash. It succeeded the lead calme or came, *q. v.*

BARGE BOARD. A false rafter set a little out from the clapboards of a gable. It protected the ends of the clapboards and concealed the underside of the roof board.

BASE. The moulded block of stone or wood on which a column, pilaster or pier directly rests. It stands upon a square block, the plinth. The mouldings vary with the order used. *See* Order.

BASE BOARD. A board of more or less width at the bottom of a wooden outside wall, or of a plastered inside wall.

BASE COURSE. An elaborately moulded base board or a stone course, plain or moulded, above the brick or stone underpinning. Moulded brick is often used.

BAT. A portion of a brick broken off and used to fill spaces. *See* Closer.

BATTEN. A board, narrow or wide, nailed on the back of two or more other boards to hold them together as in a door made of sheathing.

BATTEN DOOR. A door made in the manner described.

BEAD. A half round moulding, the same as an astragal, *q. v.*

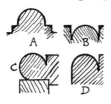

——QUIRKED. A bead at the corner of a board or of two boards. It has a quirk or sinkage on one or both sides.

——SUNK. A bead which does not project. It is necessarily quirked on both sides.

BEARER. A rather narrow beam fixed to the studs on the inside of an outer wall, to carry the ends of the second story floor joists; the device is still in use as a "ribbon" about 1⅛" by 5" or 6".

BEATER. A stick used in England and perhaps here also in early times, to "beat" mortar and thus mix the lime and sand. *See* Wren Society, volume x.

BED MOULD. A moulding beneath the soffit or "planceer," or beneath the modillion band or the dentil band, *q. v.*, of a cornice. *See* Order.

BEDROOM. This generally refers to a sleeping room on the ground floor of the house. *See* Chamber.

BELT COURSE. A course of stone, flush with the wall or projecting, or several projecting courses of brick, or a flush or projecting course of wood. Used on the outside of a building to mark the floor line or to bring about an apparent reduction in height.

BOLECTION MOULDING. A heavy moulding partly on the panel and partly on the stile or

rail of the panelwork. It was constantly used in England by Wren and is generally called, in the accounts "bolection work." It was used a good deal here before the Revolution. The derivation of the word is not known. It may possibly come from the Dutch *beleggen* akin to Ger. *belegen*, to trim or edge. Belection and balection occur, as well as bilection which appears in "a bilection plane" in a Providence inventory of 1787.

BOND. The alternation of the vertical joints in the courses of a brick or stone wall, so that these joints do not come over each other; and the laying of the bricks or stones, some across and some

BOND. (Cont'd)
lengthwise of the wall. *See* Closer.

——ENGLISH. In this form of bond, one or more courses of stretchers, or bricks laid lengthwise, are used to one course of headers, or bricks laid crosswise. *See* Closer. In later work

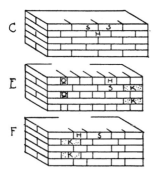

the ratio varies from one to three up to one to seven and even one to eleven. This last arrangement is hardly to be called English Bond. E.

——GARDEN WALL. An English name for three courses of stretchers to one of headers in brick work.

——FLEMISH. In this the headers and stretchers alternate in each course with the center of each header over the center of the stretcher below. F.

——COMMON. All the stones or bricks are stretchers. Used in stonework. In brick it is quite late. C.

——ALL HEADERS. Occasional in Maryland. It may have come from Western France.

BRACE. A stick set at forty-five degrees between two beams

which meet at right angles. This framing forms a triangle which will not change its shape as long as the joints hold.

——BOARDING. Outer boarding put on diagonally at the feet or tops of posts.

BRACKET. A curved or angular projection at the top of a post to enable it to support two or three beams. *See* Post Bracket, Post Flare. The scroll on the end of a step in an open-string stair.

BUTTERY. Originally bottlery (Fr. *bouteillerie*), the place where the beer and ale were distributed. Later it came to mean the same as pantry, *q. v.*

CABLE. A bead set in the low-

er third of the flute, *q. v.*, of a column or pilaster.

CAMBER. The thickening or raising of a beam in the center which is thus made higher than the ends.

CAME (*calme, calamus,* a reed). The H-shaped lead strip

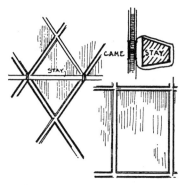

which holds the window glass. *See* Quarrel. It was made in a miniature rolling mill.

CAPITAL. The crowning member of a column or pilaster. Two forms, the Tuscan and Doric, have mouldings only, which in the Doric may be carved. The Ionic is distinguished by its volutes, of the Classic or flat type, or the angular Scamozzi form which is almost exclusively used. The Corinthian and Composite are floriated and the latter has angular volutes. The Tuscan and Composite are practically never used. *See* Order.

CARPENTER. Originally in England the workman who did the heavy framing. *See* Joiner.

CARRIAGE. The wood framing supporting the finished string and steps of a stair. *See* Stayer.

CARTOUCH. A sort of shield with scroll-work border.

CASEMENT. A frame of wood or iron filled with glass set in cames or bars and hung between mullions, to which it is hinged to swing outward. It was sometimes merely the leaded glass alone, fastened in place but not hung. Also the vertical half of a window glazing with no mullions. This swings outward on hinges and is fastened where the two halves meet in mid-opening.

CASING. The mouldings or flat strip around a door or window on the inside. *See* Architrave. In old wood-plastered partitions the frame and architrave are the same with a slight moulding.

CAVETTO (OR COVE). A hollow moulding about a quarter circle or quarter ellipse in profile. *See* Moulding.

CEILING. The underside of the floor above a room, or of a roof. An old name for sheathing, or panelling, *q. v.*

CEILING JOIST. Generally the same as collar beam, *q. v.*, but in England, and here in very rare cases, joists for the ceiling are found which are independent of the floor joists of the floor above.

CHAIR RAIL. A moulding—really a surbase, *q. v.*—carried around a room which has no panelling.

CHAMBER. A sleeping room in the second story. Probably also used for the whole second floor, as in the old expression "Up Chamber" — pronounced somewhere between chahmber and chammber—for the second story of a house.

CHAMFER. Strictly, and in its simplest form, a bevel along the edge of a beam to take off the sharp corner; (*a*) in more elabo-

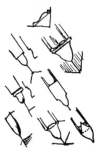

rate work it became moulded with a fillet at each corner and a quarter-round (*b*), or an ogee (*c*), between them. These ogee chamfers are sometimes four inches wide (*d*).

CHAMFER-STOP. A way of bringing the chamfer to an end before the post meets a beam or a beam meets another beam. These stops vary through the forms shown.

CHIMNEY. (Lat. *caminus*, a forge.) A fireplace and its flue. The stack above the roof of the house.

——PIECE. A wood or stone frame for a fireplace. *See* Stack. Those of wood were often carried to the ceiling.

CHYMOL. *See* Jimmer.

CLAPBOARD. A thin board a little over four feet in length riven radially, or with the grain from a "bolt", a little over four feet in length cut from a tree trunk. In early work of oak; later of pine. The word, in England about 1700, meant an unwrought barrel stave. *See* Weather Boarding.

CLOSER. Part of a brick inserted to make the joints in the alternate courses of either English or Flemish bond come over each other. A quarter of a brick, or quarter "bat" next to the first stretcher is called a queen closer. A three-quarter "bat" at the last stretcher is a king closer. *See* Bond, E, *q* and *k*.

CLOSED STRING. An outer string of a stair in which ends of the steps do not show, but which has a straight pitch from post to post. *See* String.

COIN. *See* Quoin.

COLLAR BEAM (OR COLLAR JOIST). A tie between two rafters about six feet above the garret floor. It really acts in many cases more as a brace than as a tie.

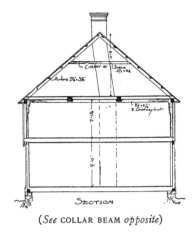

SECTION

(*See* COLLAR BEAM *opposite*)

COMMON RAFTER. A rafter reaching from the plate, *q. v.*, to the peak of the roof and supported in the middle by a purlin, *q. v. See* Truss.

CONSOLE. A scroll-shaped bracket supporting a shelf or a cornice.

COPING. The covering of a wall which carries no roof. It may be of stone, brick, or wood.

CORBEL-STEPS (Eng.), CORBIESTEPS (Scot.). The square offsets in a Dutch gable, New Amsterdam.

CORNICE. The crowning member of an entablature. It varies with the order used. Also the mouldings at the edge of the roof. These generally follow the orders. *See* also Eaves. The mouldings

of wood or plaster at the angle of wall and ceiling in a room.

COUPLES. An old word for pairs of rafters.

CROSS-GARNET. *See* Hinge.

CROSSETTE. A double mitering of the architrave at the upper corner of a door or window, or other opening.

CURB PLATE. The plate under the change of pitch in a gambrel roof.

——ROOF. *See* Gambrel.

CURTAIL STEP. The bottom step of a stair the rail of which ends in a scroll, *q. v.*, which the edge of the step follows.

CYLINDER. A modern word for the curved part of the front-string of a circular stair or a straight stair with a circular half turn. The old newel, *q. v. See* also Stair.

DADO. The plain space in a pedestal between the base and the surbase (*q. v.*). The same space in panelling. Wrongly applied to a surbase or to a chair rail, *q. v. See* Pedestal.

DENTILS. Small blocks in a classic cornice. *See* Order, Corinthian.

——BAND. A band not cut into separate dentils or, in woodwork, the band to which the dentils are nailed.

DENTICULAR. A Doric cornice which has dentils and no mutules. Seldom used unless for inside work. Neither Batty Langley, 1741, nor Paine 1794, show it.

DOG-LEGGED STAIR. One type of solid-newel stair, *q. v.*

DOME. A roof of wood or a ceiling of plaster generally in the form of a half or a smaller segment of a sphere. Sometimes octagonal in plan with a pointed section.

DORMER. A vertical window in the slope of a roof. *See* Lutheran. Luthern occurs as late as 1827 in Worcester's American edition of Walker's Johnson.

DORMANT TREE. An old name for a summer, *q. v.*

DOVETAIL. The end of a beam cut into a truncated wedge to prevent it from pulling out of the framing.

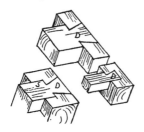

——HALF. One side of a beam cut as a wedge while the other is straight.

——SHOULDERED. Where part of the dovetailed beam is let into its supporter.

DOWEL. A piece of hard wood used to hold two boards together.

DRAGON BEAM. A diagonal summer pojecting over an outer

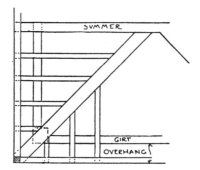

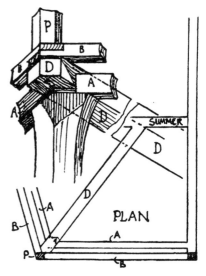

corner of a house to carry an overhang.

DRAW-BORE TENON. A tenon in which the pinhole does not align with that in the cheeks or sides of the mortise, but is kept nearer the inside of the mortised beam so that when the pin is driven it has to drag the shoulders of the tenon close against the mortised beam or post. This is apt to cause difficulty in the proper taking down of old work which is to be set up again, as the oak pins may be found so bent that they cannot be "drifted," or driven out.

DRIPSTONE. A ledge in a chimney just above the slope of the roof and sometimes also just above the ridge, to prevent water from following the face of the masonry into the house.

EASE. A curve in a handrail connecting a descending rail to the post cap at its foot.

EAVES. The projection of rafters, boarding and shingles beyond the face of the wall below. The early form of watershed which preceded the classic form of cornice with its mouldings.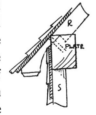

EGG AND DART. Also called Egg and Tongue. An ornament

applied to the ovolo or quarter-round moulding, *q. v.*

ENGLISH BOND. A course of headers alternating with a course of stretchers. *See* Bond, English; Closer.

ENTABLATURE. The whole weight or superstructure carried

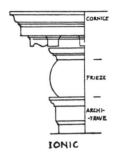

IONIC

by the columns or pilasters of an order. It consists of architrave, frieze, and cornice, *q. v.*

ENTASIS. The curve of the line in which a column diminishes in diameter as it rises.

ENTRY. The space into which outside door of a house opened. It might be a space in front of the stairs and chimney, or it might be what is now called a hall running from front to back of the house. It is a remnant of the "screens" of an old English house.

EXTRADOS. The line of the backs of the voussoirs of an arch. *See* Arch, Intrados, Voussoir.

FASCIA. A flat band. One of the divisions of an Ionic or Corinthian architrave, *q. v.*

FEATHEREDGED. Brought to a sharp edge, triangular in sec-

FEATHEREDGED. (Cont'd) tion, as in one side of a clapboard or in the sides of a panel or one or more sides of a sheathing board. *See* Bolection Moulding, Panel.

FESTOONS. Drapery or flowers carved as drooping on the

place to keep the brick or stone from burning out.

FIREPLACE. The space in the chimney stack where the actual fire is built. It consists of the floor which has the hearth in front and the underfire behind, the jambs at

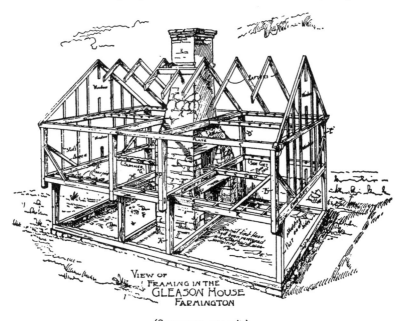

VIEW OF FRAMING IN THE GLEASON HOUSE FARMINGTON

(See FRAME *opposite*)

walls as if hung at intervals from ornamental supports.

FILLET. A small square member between two mouldings or between a moulding and a wider flat surface. A small projecting strip. One of the narrow vertical divisions separating the flutes of a column or pilaster.

FIREBACK. A cast-iron plate set up against the back of a fire-

the sides, which are sometimes set at right angles to the back, with a square corner or a quadrant, but most often set on a bevel.

——COUNT RUMFORD. Triangular in plan. *See* Rumford.

FLARE. A modern word to describe a post which, instead of having a bracket, *q. v.*, at its top increases in size throughout its whole height. *See* Post Flare.

FLEMISH BOND. Headers and stretchers alternating in the same course. *See* Bond, F, Closer.

FLUSH. Surfaces which, whether continuous or not, are in the same plane.

FLUTE. A vertical hollow, in a series decorating the surface of a column or pilaster.

FLYERS. Steps set at right angles to the axis of a stair, in distinction from winders, *q. v. See* Stair.

FOOTPACE. A considerable space set lengthwise in a straight flight of stairs, as a resting place. *See* Stair, Half-Pace, H, and Quarter Pace, Q.

FRAME. The assemblage of light and heavy timbers which carried the covering and filling of sides, floors and roof. *See also* Summer. The head jambs and sill, *q. v.*, put together, to form a door or window opening.

(*See illustration opposite*)

FRET. A pattern jig-sawed out of thin wood and applied to a surface.

FRIEZE. The second or middle member, in height, of an entablature. It rests on the architrave and carries the cornice.

——CUSHION. A convex face given to the frieze by Palladio and handed on by Batty Langley and William Pain. *See* Order, Ionic.

FROW, FROE. A tool with the blade set at right angles to the handle. Its edge was on the bottom of the blade, the back of

which was struck with a mallet or a maul. It was used by coopers to rive barrel staves and by carpenters in getting out the old riven laths and clapboards.

FURRING. Bringing the faces of joists or studs into line with each other by nailing on thin strips of wood.

GABLE. The outline of the wall at the end of a roof from the eaves or cornice to the peak or ridge.

GAIN. A space cut out of a post to relieve the tenon of a girt, or cut from a girt to receive the end of a stud.

GALLETING. Inserting small stones, black or dark blue, in the wide mortar joints of a stone underpinning.

GAMBREL. A form of roof in two slopes on each side, the lower slopes steep like an early roof, the upper rather flat. Probably de-

GAMBREL. (Cont'd)
rived from the French Mansard,
so called, and used for the same

purpose, to prevent an enormous
height of the steep roof in the
wide houses of the later type.

GARRET. The story under the
roof and above the second story.
In a story-and-a-half house it
would still be called the chamber.

GAUGED. Used to describe
brick cut to fit in an arch ring, or
shaped to a pattern by cutting
instead of by moulding. It is also
used of the plaster of Paris added
to lime for finishing plaster, and
to lime building mortar also, formerly, to make it set more rapidly.

GEMMELS. *See* Chymol, Jimmer, Hinge.

GIMMER. *See* Jimmer.

GIRT. A beam in the outer
wall of a building to receive the
ends of the floor joists. It carries
the summer when the latter does
not rest on a post. *See* Frame,
Summer.

GOOSENECK. A workman's
term for a ramp, *q. v.*

GORGE. A hollow moulding,
the same as the cove or cavetto,
q. v.

GROUNDSILL (GRUNDSILL,
GRUNSEL). An old name for the
sill, *q. v.*, also Frame.

GUTTER. A 6 x 10 or there-
abouts, hollowed out is sometimes
found as a part of the main cornice, where it serves as does the
familiar wooden dug-out gutter.

HALF-PACE. The landing in
a double-run stair where a half
turn is made. *See* Quarter-Pace,
Footpace.

HALF-ROUND. The Torus
moulding. *See* Moulding.

HALL. The living room and
kitchen of a one-room seventeenth-century house. When the
kitchen was moved into a lean-to
or was in the cellar, it retained
its name. It was the descendant of
the old English hall and was never
a passageway. Sometimes called
fire room in one-room houses.

HALL CHAMBER. The room
above the hall.

HAND RAIL. The rail of a
stair.

HEAD. The lintel or top-piece
of a door or window frame. *See*
Jamb.

HEADERS. Bricks laid across
the wall so that their ends show.
See Bond.

HEADING COURSE. A
course all headers.

HERRINGBONE WORK.

Bricks laid at an angle of forty-five degrees.

HINGE. The mechanism for hanging doors to swing.

——LOOP. Two bent pieces of metal looped together. Mostly

used in old chests, they sometimes have survived in houses.

——SNIBELL. This is the true hinge. A long bar sometimes with a well-wrought outer end

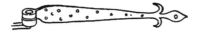

and an inner end formed as an eye which went over a snibell (possibly snipe bill), a word now superseded by "pintle."

——JIMMER. From old Fr. *jumel* (*jumeau*) a twin. An inseparable hinge. The snibell form could be taken apart, since the door could be lifted off. With the jimmer the hinge must be taken from the frame to release the door.

——VARIANTS OF THE JIMMER.

Cock's Head.

Cross Garnet. T-shaped

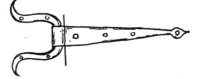

with the head on the jamb. Sometimes quite ornate.

H hinge.

HL hinge. Pew door H.

HIP (OR HIPPED) ROOF. A roof which pitches from all four walls of the building it covers.

HIP. An external angle formed by the meeting of two roof sur-

faces of a hip roof. The opposite of a valley, *q. v.*

HIP-GAMBREL. A combination of a gambrel and a hip roof

HIP-GAMBREL. (Cont'd) with the two small gables of the gambrel. Very common in Newport. It seems rare elsewhere.

IMPOST. A horizontal block, plain or moulded, from which an arch springs.

INTRADOS. The under side of the ring of voussoirs forming an arch. *See* Voussoir, Extrados.

ITALIAN MOULDING. The wide heavy moulding surrounding a fireplace opening in early panel-

ing. So called in Wren's time. It came to us from England which it reached from Italy through France.

JAMB. The side of a window or door frame, of an opening in a wall, or of a fireplace.

JERKIN-HEAD. The truncation, or bevelling off, of a gable.

JET. A carpenter's word for a cornice. An overhang.

JETTY. An overhang, *q. v.*

JIMMER. Literally a twin, Old Fr. *jumel* (*jumeau*). A hinge the parts of which are not separable. *See* Hinge, Chymol, Gemmel, Gimmer.

JOINER. A carpenter who did inside finish and panelling. A cabinet maker. Older signs used to read "Carpenter and Joiner." *See* Carpenter.

JOINTER. A long plane for truing up the edges of boards.

JOISTS. The smaller beams which directly supported the floor between the girts and the summer. Later they spanned the whole room from girt to girt. *See* Frame, Summer

KEYSTONE. A voussoir in the center of the arch ring, made longer than the others. It is often carved, sometimes has side pieces, and is sometimes shaped with side scrolls. It is so called because it is set last and closes the arch. *See* Arch.

KING POST. A post which originally in mediaeval work stood on a heavy beam and actually supported the upper ends of the rafters. It has long been really a tie which hangs from the peak of the roof and supports the tie beam. *See* Truss, Queen Post.

KNEE. A bracket, generally rectangular, made out of a naturally bent limb of a tree. Generally used to tie a corner horizontally. *See* Rafter, Knee.

LANTERN. A structure square, octagonal or round in plan, sometimes of considerable height, set on a roof generally as an observation point, but often for mere appearance, or on a dome to give light. The sides may be open or glazed at pleasure.

A short stage in a steeple consisting of the belfry as at Christ Church, Cambridge; or of the belfry with a short stage above it.

LATCH. A contrivance of wood or metal for keeping a door closed. It consists of a bar and a keeper; with a means of raising the bar and a means of pulling the door open or shut.

LATCHSTRING. A piece of raw hide fastened to the bar of a wooden latch and carried through the door so as to hang free on the outside. By pulling it down the bar could be raised, but with the string on the inside the door could not be opened.

LEAN-TO. A room or line of rooms with a roof which seems to

lean against a larger mass. A house with such a roof at its back.

LIGHTS. The panes of glass in a window as an eight-"light", or twelve-"light" window. In early times the open spaces between the mullions, q. v., of a two-, three-, or four-"light" window.

LINTEL. A heavy beam of stone or wood over an opening.

LOCK, BOX. An iron mechanism encased in a wood or iron case which was fastened to a rail of the door.

LOCK RAIL. A horizontal strip or rail between the panels of a door above mid-height. It was of considerable width to receive on its face the usual box lock which was applied to it.

LUTHERAN WINDOW. Luthorn, Luthern (Fr. *lucarne*). A dormer window, *q. v.*

MANTEL. Originally a wood-and-plaster or a stone hood, later a vertical wall over the fireplace. The eighteenth-century English word for what we know as a mantel is chimney piece, *q. v. See also* Italian moulding.

MANTLETREE. A heavy oak beam over the fireplace opening to carry the masonry above. It is always chamfered in early work and sometimes moulded.

METOPE. The space between two triglyphs in the frieze of the Doric order. *See* Order, Doric; and Triglyph.

MODILLION. A form of bracket in the cornice of the Corinthian and Composite orders, and of Palladio's and Scamozzi's Ionic.

MORTISE. A rectangular sinkage in a beam to receive a tenon,

MORTISE. (Cont'd)
q. v., cut on the end of another beam. The pin or treenail driven through both beams ties them together.

MOULDING. An ornamental shaping of the internal or external angles or surfaces or of the faces of a beam board, or other solid, or of a group of these, into forms copied from those used in stone-

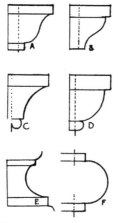

work. The usual forms are shown in the illustration: (a) Cyma Recta, Cyma, or Crownmould; (b) Cyma Reversa or Ogee; (c) Cavetto or Cove; (d) Ovolo or Quarter Round; (e) Scotia or Hollow; (f) Torus or half round. See also Astragal, Bead.

MULLION. An upright piece of wood, generally moulded in early work, and rebated and beaded later, which divided the lights, q. v., of a casement window. See Window, Mullioned.

MUNTIN. The strip of wood separating the panes of a sash or casement. The same as a bar, q. v.

MUTULE. A sort of flat bracket in the mutular Doric Order. See Order, Doric.

NEWEL. To-day, in this country this means the lowest post of the stair, that at the start. The others are called intermediates. Anciently it meant the post around which a circular stair wound in its ascent. Later the word came to mean the opening or open space around which the stair rose, whether this space was square, circular, or elliptical. This was called an open newel while the post around which the corkscrew stair rose was called a closed newel. The colonial planners generally employed the open newel. It seems impossible now to tell when the modern meaning, that of the lowest post, came into use. See Stair.

NOSING. The rounded projection of the tread of a step beyond the face of the riser or of the string.

OGEE. The cyma reversa moulding, convex above and concave below. See Moulding.

ORDER. The definite arrangement of a column and its load or entablature. There are technically five of these: Tuscan, Doric, Ionic, Corinthian and Composite. Prac-

IONIC

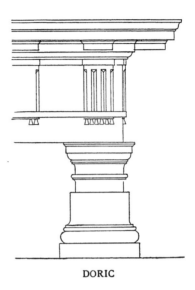

DORIC

CORINTHIAN

ORDER. (Cont'd)

tically there are but three for the Tuscan is a clumsy Doric and the Composite is a fusion of the Corinthian and the angular Ionic. It would be hard to find Tuscan or Composite in Colonial work.

——TUSCAN. This has few distinguishing features.

——DORIC. Both mutular and denticular have triglyphs, *q. v.*, but our ancestors often omitted mutules and triglyphs.

——IONIC. The classic Ionic has a capital with volutes which are set parallel to the architrave above. The Scamozzi type, so-called, which is really of ancient origin, is the prevalent form in Colonial work. It has volutes turned outward at an angle of forty-five degrees. This was really an ancient form preferred because all four of its sides looked alike. With this order Palladio used a cushion frieze, *q. v.* Both Palladio and Scamozzi used modillions in the cornice though the classic form does not.

——CORINTHIAN. Here the capital has two rows of leaves and there are small volutes under the corners of the abacus which has curved sides in plan. The entablature is plain except for carving. There are modillions in the cornice.

——COMPOSITE. Here the Corinthian leaves are joined to the volutes of the angular Ionic. The cornice has no modillions.

OVERHANG. The projection

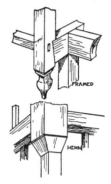

of one story beyond that below. *See* Jetty.

——FRAMED. With separate posts.

——HEWN. With continuous posts.

OVOLO. The quarter-round moulding. *See* Moulding.

PACE. A platform. *See* Footpace, Half-pace, Quarter-pace.

PALLADIAN WINDOW. This name seems to be late. *See* Venetian window.

PANEL. In woodwork a board planed to a featheredge. Each of its four sides is set into a frame of stiles and rails, *q. v.*, or into a bolection mould-ing, *q. v.* The panel itself may be plain, or raised-and-bevelled, or raised-beaded-and-bevelled. It may also be plain with mouldings planted on its face.

PANEL BACK. A panel under a window sill, inside the house.

PANELLING. A series of panels: (*a*) over the whole room; (*b*) over the whole fireplace end; (*c*) around the room up to the windows or higher, or a combination of *b* and *c*. Panelled ceilings occur.

PANTRY (Fr. *pain*). The place where the bread and dry provisions were kept.

PARLOR. Originally a room in a monastery where conversation was allowed. The withdrawing room—"company room" of the house, across the entry from the hall.

PARLOR CHAMBER. The bedroom above the parlor.

PEDESTAL. A moulded block, with base, dado or die, and surbase, which was set beneath a column or pilaster. Usually seen in mantelpieces and outside doorways of the early eighteenth century.

PEDIMENT. A gable of moderate pitch with the cornice carried across at its base, and up the raking sides. It may be triangular, segmental, broken or "scrolled" in various ways.

PIER. The mass of masonry at each side of an arch. A mass of masonry to support a large beam.

PILASTER. A flat, slightly projecting mass doing duty as a column and given all the details of the latter.

PIN. A round piece of hard wood used to fasten mortises and tenons together. In the panel work they were usually pine. In frames of oak they were somewhat roughly made to prevent turning in the joint. *See* Draw-Bore Tenon. Large pins were called treenails, *q. v.*

PITCH. The ratio of the rise of a roof to its span, as one third pitch. The rise in a given number of feet.

PLANCER (PLANCEER). (Fr. *plancher*.) The soffit of a cornice, *q. v.* "Plancer" can still be heard among carpenters.

PLASTER CORNICE. On the outside these are fairly early and take the form of a plastered cove. *See* Rafter, Knee. On the inside they appear with the Adams and Asher Benjamin.

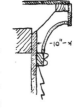

PLATE. The beam framed on the tops of the posts to carry the common rafters and to tie the house lengthwise. *See* Frame, Summer.

POST. A heavy upright piece of timber set at each corner of the building, and at intervals between, to carry the girts and the plates and through them the floors and the roof. The posts are framed into the sills and the plates and the girts are framed into the posts. *See* Frame, Summer.

POST BRACKET. A projec-

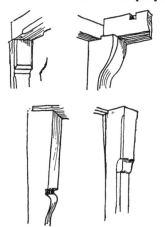

tion at the head of a post to enlarge the bearing space.

POST FLARE. A straight or

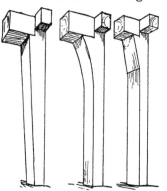

curved enlargement of a post, from the floor up, to do the work of the post brackets while saving a goodly amount of hewing.

PURLIN. A beam framed between the principal rafters on

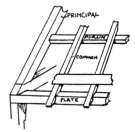

each side of a roof to carry the common rafters or simply vertical boarding.

——ROOF. A roof boarded vertically directly on purlins with no common rafters.

QUARREL. A lozenge-shaped piece of glass set in lead "cames," *q. v.*

QUARTER. *See* Stud.

QUARTER GRAIN. Wood sawed or riven parallel to the grain, "grainway" in modern parlance. Used mostly of oak, as quartered oak. *See* Wainscot.

QUARTER-PACE. The corner landing in a stair with three runs, *q. v. See* Pace.

QUEEN POST. A vertical post, one of a pair, in a truss over a wide span. It, like the King post, *q. v.*, is really a tie. *See* Truss.

QUIRK. A cutting back of the upper part of a moulding under

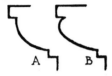

the fillet. This form, except in the bead, is characteristic of Asher Benjamin's time. It is shown at B in the cut, a quirked ovolo while A gives the regular form. *See also* Bead, Quirked.

QUOINS. Square stones set at the corners of a brick or stone

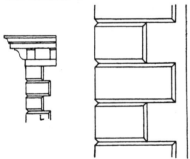

building. Imitation of these in woodwork.

RABBET (REBATE). A rectangular sinkage at the corner of a piece of framing or finish, generally to receive another piece joined thereto.

RAFTER (PRINCIPAL). The beam forming the slope of a roof truss, *q. v.*

——COMMON. One of the smaller beams which run over the purlins, *q. v.*, from plate to ridge and carry the roof boarding.

——KNEE OR BENT TREE PRINCIPAL. A principal rafter so cut

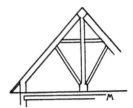

from a tree branch as to have at its foot a bend or "knee" which comes down on the plate at a right angle as is shown in the cut from Moxon (M). The object was to provide for a plastered cove cornice without an extra plate, as is shown in

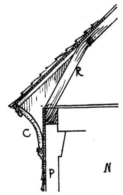

the sketch (N) from an actual example in Newport. This is perhaps the last descendant of the old English "Curved Tree Principal," shown by Mr. C. E. Innocent in his *Development of*

RAFTER. (Cont'd)
English Building Construction, ch. iv, figures 8 and 9.

RAIL. The horizonatal pieces carrying the panels in doors and other panelwork. The sloping or horizontal bar which guards the side of a stair well or other opening.

RAKE. A slope, as of a gable, or a stair string.

RAKING CORNICE. The cornice along the rake or slope of a gable or pediment. *See* Barge Board, Pediment.

RAMP. The upward turn of a stair rail to bring it to a mitre

with the level rail above. The opposite of an ease. Often called by workmen a "gooseneck."

READER'S DESK. The middle compartment of a "three-decker" pulpit, *q. v.*

REEDING. A series of convexities, like a bundle of reeds, the opposite of flutes, used in place of the latter in columns and pilasters and elsewhere.

RETURN. To carry a moulding around a corner against the surface from which it projects. Also used of the part of the moulding so treated.

RIDGE. The peak of a roof, the line of the tops of the rafter joints.

RIDGEPOLE. A small beam into which the tops of the rafters are framed. Very rare.

RIFT. Wood split or sawed with the grain. *See* Quarter Grain, Riven.

RISE. The height of a stair step from tread to tread.

RISER. The vertical board at the front of a step.

RIVEN. Split as in old clapboards, and some early plank. *See* Rift, Frow. *Cf.* the *geklofte eik* of the Plymouth fort.

RUBBED BRICK. Brick rubbed to give them a smoother surface and a lighter color. Common in Virginia.

RUBBLE. Field stone or roughly quarried stone, shaped with the hammer.

RUMFORD FIREPLACE. Invented by Count Rumford. Triangular in plan it throws more heat into the room than the common type, partly, perhaps, because the fire itself is brought further forward.

RUSTICATION. An emphasis of the joints in the stone work of walls by a square or V-shaped sinkage. The same treatment is also imitated in woodwork.

SASH (Shas. Fr. *chasser*). A wooden frame filled with leaded glass, or with glass set in wooden bars or muntins. There are two sash in a window and the lower sash is movable up and down. It differs from a casement in having this vertical motion while a casement swings out. It appears in England at Whitehall in 1685.

SASH WEIGHT. A mass of metal, probably lead, to counterweight the sash.

SAW PIT. A pit over which the log to be sawed was laid and in which the "pit man" stood at the lower end of the vertical "pit saw" while the "top sawyer" stood over the log above.

SCOTIA (OR HOLLOW). A moulding the reverse of the Torus, *q. v.*

SCROLL. A spiral turn at the end of a stair rail at the beginning of the lowest run.

SHEATHING. Boards one inch thick, or even less, generally of pine, soft or hard, but sometimes of whitewood or chestnut or even of oak. The boards are set vertically or horizontally—the latter is usual on the side and end walls of studded houses. The edges of the boards are moulded, or are feathered, for the joints

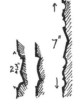

and narrow boards are inserted between the wide ones at intervals.

SHIPLAPPING. Shaving the ends of clapboards and bevelling

the edges of outside boarding to keep out water.

SHUTTER. A solid blind, used inside or outside. The early inside shutter slid in a groove or on a track on the window stool and its continuation, the chair rail. Later the shutter was hung double on each side as in England.

SHUTTER BOX. A space or pocket on each side of a window to receive the folded double-hung shutters.

SILL. The heavy timber on the foundation of a building. It carried the posts and studs of the walls, and the framing of the first floor as well. *See* Frame, Ground Sill. The bottom crosspiece of a window frame. *See* Stool Casing. A threshold.

SLITWORK. Sawing three-inch plank, or even one-inch boards lengthwise to reduce their thickness to one inch or even one half inch.

SOFFIT. The underside of a projection, as a cornice, or of an architrave. *See* Plancer. Also used of the intrados, *q. v.*, of a vault, *q. v.*

SPIRE. The staged and pointed portion of a steeple above the tower.

STACK OF CHIMNEYS. What we understand by chimney —the whole mass fireplace, flues, and outside stack. 1662.

STAFF BEAD. The moulding around a window or door frame in a brick wall, close to the brickwork, to stop water.

STAIR. A succession of steps leading from one floor to the next above or below.

——BLOCK STEP OR SOLID STEP. Two parallel sloping beams— the "pair of stayers" to which

are pinned sections of wood beams split or sawed on their diagonals. A few cellar stairs of this type have been found.

——SOLID NEWEL.

Dog-leg. In this type the strings, with the rail and balusters are over each other, so that there is only one post at the turn and thus no open well.

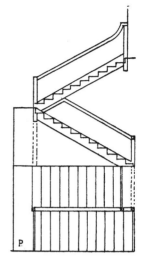

Zig-Zag. Box steps alternately on one side and the other between walls.

——OPEN NEWEL. Square or rectangular plan. *See* Scroll.

Circular or Oval Plan. These, except for the cir-

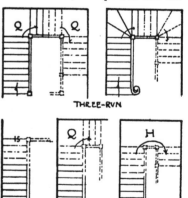

THREE-RUN

ONE-RUN   TWO — RUN

One-run.   Two-run.
Three-run.

cular stair in the Old State House in Boston, are really Post-Colonial.

Half circle joining two runs.

Continuous curve, all winders.

Right-hand.

Left-hand. With the rail of the balustrade on the right or left in ascending.

STAYER. *See* Stair, Block Step.

STEEPLE. The combination of tower and spire.

STEP. Originally a block of stone on a masonry foundation; or a short beam bevelled and fastened to two "stayers." *See* Stair, Block Step. Later steps were built up of a horizontal board for the tread and a vertical board for the riser.

STEP BRACKET. An ornament on the string at the end of a step, jig-sawed or carved, often very elaborately.

STILE. The vertical strip at the side of a panel and between two panels. *See* Rail.

STOOL CASING. The flat member with the moulding and "apron" below it on the inside of the sill of a window.

STRING. The support of the steps of a stair.

——OUTSIDE OR FRONT. May be a "closed" or "box" string which is of one width through-out and is moulded and shows no steps, or an "open" string which is cut out for the steps the ends of which are thus clearly defined. The former type is the older.

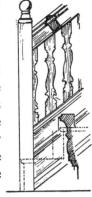

——WALL. The finished string against the wall.

STUD. The upright stick, roughly 3 x 4, which, in a stud house, fills the spaces between the sills, posts, girts and plate. It is an old English provincial word which came over with the settlers. The usual English word for what we still call a "stud" is "quarter."

SUMMER. The heavy beam which crosses the ceiling of a room from girt to girt and carries the joists of the floor above.

——LENGTHWISE. Parallel with the front wall of the house.

——THWARTWISE. Parallel with the end wall and thus at right angles with the front wall.

——DIAGONAL. *See* Dragon Beam.

——CROSSED. A lengthwise and thwartwise summer framed together in mid ceiling. Several examples exist.

(See illustrations on next page)

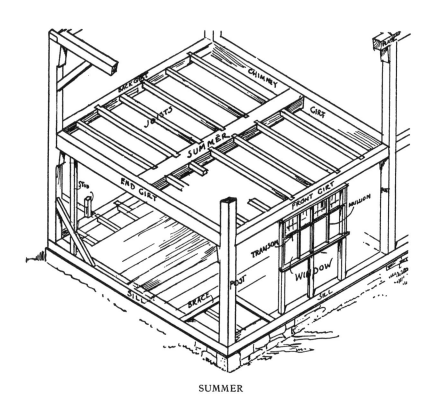

SUMMER

CROSSED SUMMER

SURBASE. The upper moulding of a Pedestal, *q. v.*, or of low panelling, or carried around without panels.

TENON. A short projection from the end of a beam. It is pinned into a mortise, *q. v.* See *also* Tusk.

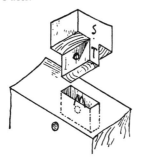

THATCH. Coarse grass used for roofing as in England.

THREE-DECKER. A common name for an early pulpit,

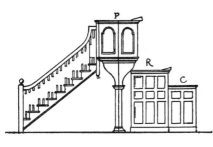

with its three parts, Pulpit, Reader's desk, *q. v.*, and "Clark's" desk.

TIE BEAM. A beam connecting the feet of the principal rafters of a truss to prevent them from spreading. In the ordinary houses the girts in the third floor act as ties.

TORUS. A moulding whic his a half-round or a little more, in section. *See* Moulding.

TRANSOM. A piece of wood framed between or across the mullions of a window, or across an arched window or door. *See* Mullioned Window.

TREENAILS. Pins used in framing.

TRIGLYPH. A slightly projecting rectangular slab in the Doric frieze.

TRUSS.

RAFTERS AND TIE BEAM

RAFTER TIE AND COLLAR

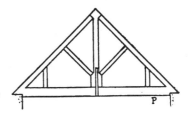

KING-POST TRUSS (P-Pain)

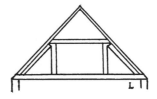

QUEEN-POST TRUSS (L-Langley)

TRUSS. (Cont'd)

Essentially a triangle formed by two rafters and a tie beam, *q. v.*, for the support of a roof with or without collar joist. To this may be added a king post, *q. v.*, or two queen posts, *q. v.*, and certain braces.

TUSK TENON. A sort of

tenon with one sloping shoulder used in early floor joist.

TUSK AND TENON. A tenon

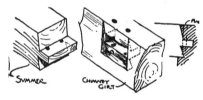

with a tusk below it, used in large beams.

TYPE. An old word, common in Wren's time and even much later, for the sounding board of a pulpit.

UNDERPINNING. The stone or brick wall which rose a foot or more above the ground to support a wooden building—where there was no cellar it was generally only "shovel deep." When there was a cellar it stood on the cellar wall and formed a continuation thereof.

VALLEY. The re-entrant angle formed by the meeting of two roof-slopes, the ridges of which

are at right angles. Two parallel roofs, the eaves whereof meet, also form a valley, at the bottom. Such construction was used in England and not unknown here.

VAULT. A ceiling arched in various ways.

——I. BARREL VAULT. A continuous arch for the length of the room.

——2. DOMICAL VAULT. A dome, generally quite flat.

——3. GROINED VAULT. Formed by the intersection of two cylinders.

VENETIAN DOOR. In England, a door with sidelights. *See* Window, Venetian.

VOUSSOIR. One of the wedge-shaped stones or one of the bricks of which the ring of an arch is built.

WAINSCOT. Originally this meant quartered oak. It was later transferred to the panelling made of it. Our ancestors used it to mean sheathing or ceiling (seal-ing). *See* Winthrop's rebuke to Ludlow in his Journal.

WATER TABLE. A slope, plain or moulded, at the top of the underpinning or at the first floor level or offset.

WEATHER BOARDING. Wide boards, bevelled on one edge, and lapped like clapboards.

WELL HOLE. The opening around which a stair run is built, an open newel. *See* Newel.

WIND BRACE. A brace from a principal rafter to a purlin.

WINDERS. Steps with radi-ating risers and thus narrowing treads. *See* Flyers.

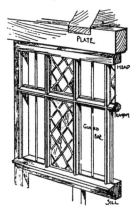

WINDOW.
——SINGLE. One opening.

——MULLIONED. Divided by mul-lions into two or more lights.

——CASEMENT. With glazed frames swinging out.

——TRANSOM. With a horizontal division, with or without mul-lions.

——SASH. (Fr. *chasse*). With sash sliding up and down.

——VENETIAN (*Vernition*). A group of three windows. The central one is wider and taller

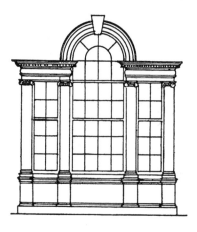

than the rest and is round-headed. The two side windows are square-headed. *See* Palla-dian. Perhaps any window with sidelights and an elliptical top-light. *See* Venetian Door.

A CATALOG OF SELECTED DOVER
BOOKS IN ALL FIELDS OF INTEREST

CONCERNING THE SPIRITUAL IN ART, Wassily Kandinsky. Pioneering work by father of abstract art. Thoughts on color theory, nature of art. Analysis of earlier masters. 12 illustrations. 80pp. of text. 5⅜ x 8½.   0-486-23411-8

CELTIC ART: The Methods of Construction, George Bain. Simple geometric techniques for making Celtic interlacements, spirals, Kells-type initials, animals, humans, etc. Over 500 illustrations. 160pp. 9 x 12. (Available in U.S. only.)   0-486-22923-8

AN ATLAS OF ANATOMY FOR ARTISTS, Fritz Schider. Most thorough reference work on art anatomy in the world. Hundreds of illustrations, including selections from works by Vesalius, Leonardo, Goya, Ingres, Michelangelo, others. 593 illustrations. 192pp. 7⅛ x 10¼.   0-486-20241-0

CELTIC HAND STROKE-BY-STROKE (Irish Half-Uncial from "The Book of Kells"): An Arthur Baker Calligraphy Manual, Arthur Baker. Complete guide to creating each letter of the alphabet in distinctive Celtic manner. Covers hand position, strokes, pens, inks, paper, more. Illustrated. 48pp. 8¼ x 11.   0-486-24336-2

EASY ORIGAMI, John Montroll. Charming collection of 32 projects (hat, cup, pelican, piano, swan, many more) specially designed for the novice origami hobbyist. Clearly illustrated easy-to-follow instructions insure that even beginning papercrafters will achieve successful results. 48pp. 8¼ x 11.   0-486-27298-2

BLOOMINGDALE'S ILLUSTRATED 1886 CATALOG: Fashions, Dry Goods and Housewares, Bloomingdale Brothers. Famed merchants' extremely rare catalog depicting about 1,700 products: clothing, housewares, firearms, dry goods, jewelry, more. Invaluable for dating, identifying vintage items. Also, copyright-free graphics for artists, designers. Co-published with Henry Ford Museum & Greenfield Village. 160pp. 8¼ x 11.   0-486-25780-0

THE ART OF WORLDLY WISDOM, Baltasar Gracian. "Think with the few and speak with the many," "Friends are a second existence," and "Be able to forget" are among this 1637 volume's 300 pithy maxims. A perfect source of mental and spiritual refreshment, it can be opened at random and appreciated either in brief or at length. 128pp. 5⅜ x 8½.   0-486-44034-6

JOHNSON'S DICTIONARY: A Modern Selection, Samuel Johnson (E. L. McAdam and George Milne, eds.). This modern version reduces the original 1755 edition's 2,300 pages of definitions and literary examples to a more manageable length, retaining the verbal pleasure and historical curiosity of the original. 480pp. 5³⁄₁₆ x 8¼.   0-486-44089-3

ADVENTURES OF HUCKLEBERRY FINN, Mark Twain, Illustrated by E. W. Kemble. A work of eternal richness and complexity, a source of ongoing critical debate, and a literary landmark, Twain's 1885 masterpiece about a barefoot boy's journey of self-discovery has enthralled readers around the world. This handsome clothbound reproduction of the first edition features all 174 of the original black-and-white illustrations. 368pp. 5⅜ x 8½.   0-486-44322-1

STICKLEY CRAFTSMAN FURNITURE CATALOGS, Gustav Stickley and L. & J. G. Stickley. Beautiful, functional furniture in two authentic catalogs from 1910. 594 illustrations, including 277 photos, show settles, rockers, armchairs, reclining chairs, bookcases, desks, tables. 183pp. 6½ x 9¼. 0-486-23838-5

AMERICAN LOCOMOTIVES IN HISTORIC PHOTOGRAPHS: 1858 to 1949, Ron Ziel (ed.). A rare collection of 126 meticulously detailed official photographs, called "builder portraits," of American locomotives that majestically chronicle the rise of steam locomotive power in America. Introduction. Detailed captions. xi+ 129pp. 9 x 12. 0-486-27393-8

AMERICA'S LIGHTHOUSES: An Illustrated History, Francis Ross Holland, Jr. Delightfully written, profusely illustrated fact-filled survey of over 200 American lighthouses since 1716. History, anecdotes, technological advances, more. 240pp. 8 x 10¾. 0-486-25576-X

TOWARDS A NEW ARCHITECTURE, Le Corbusier. Pioneering manifesto by founder of "International School." Technical and aesthetic theories, views of industry, economics, relation of form to function, "mass-production split" and much more. Profusely illustrated. 320pp. 6⅛ x 9¼. (Available in U.S. only.) 0-486-25023-7

HOW THE OTHER HALF LIVES, Jacob Riis. Famous journalistic record, exposing poverty and degradation of New York slums around 1900, by major social reformer. 100 striking and influential photographs. 233pp. 10 x 7⅞. 0-486-22012-5

FRUIT KEY AND TWIG KEY TO TREES AND SHRUBS, William M. Harlow. One of the handiest and most widely used identification aids. Fruit key covers 120 deciduous and evergreen species; twig key 160 deciduous species. Easily used. Over 300 photographs. 126pp. 5⅜ x 8½. 0-486-20511-8

COMMON BIRD SONGS, Dr. Donald J. Borror. Songs of 60 most common U.S. birds: robins, sparrows, cardinals, bluejays, finches, more—arranged in order of increasing complexity. Up to 9 variations of songs of each species.
Cassette and manual 0-486-99911-4

ORCHIDS AS HOUSE PLANTS, Rebecca Tyson Northen. Grow cattleyas and many other kinds of orchids—in a window, in a case, or under artificial light. 63 illustrations. 148pp. 5⅜ x 8½. 0-486-23261-1

MONSTER MAZES, Dave Phillips. Masterful mazes at four levels of difficulty. Avoid deadly perils and evil creatures to find magical treasures. Solutions for all 32 exciting illustrated puzzles. 48pp. 8¼ x 11. 0-486-26005-4

MOZART'S DON GIOVANNI (DOVER OPERA LIBRETTO SERIES), Wolfgang Amadeus Mozart. Introduced and translated by Ellen H. Bleiler. Standard Italian libretto, with complete English translation. Convenient and thoroughly portable—an ideal companion for reading along with a recording or the performance itself. Introduction. List of characters. Plot summary. 121pp. 5¼ x 8½. 0-486-24944-1

FRANK LLOYD WRIGHT'S DANA HOUSE, Donald Hoffmann. Pictorial essay of residential masterpiece with over 160 interior and exterior photos, plans, elevations, sketches and studies. 128pp. 9¼ x 10¾. 0-486-29120-0

THE CLARINET AND CLARINET PLAYING, David Pino. Lively, comprehensive work features suggestions about technique, musicianship, and musical interpretation, as well as guidelines for teaching, making your own reeds, and preparing for public performance. Includes an intriguing look at clarinet history. "A godsend," *The Clarinet,* Journal of the International Clarinet Society. Appendixes. 7 illus. 320pp. 5⅜ x 8½. 0-486-40270-3

HOLLYWOOD GLAMOR PORTRAITS, John Kobal (ed.). 145 photos from 1926-49. Harlow, Gable, Bogart, Bacall; 94 stars in all. Full background on photographers, technical aspects. 160pp. 8⅜ x 11¼. 0-486-23352-9

THE RAVEN AND OTHER FAVORITE POEMS, Edgar Allan Poe. Over 40 of the author's most memorable poems: "The Bells," "Ulalume," "Israfel," "To Helen," "The Conqueror Worm," "Eldorado," "Annabel Lee," many more. Alphabetic lists of titles and first lines. 64pp. 5$\frac{3}{16}$ x 8¼. 0-486-26685-0

PERSONAL MEMOIRS OF U. S. GRANT, Ulysses Simpson Grant. Intelligent, deeply moving firsthand account of Civil War campaigns, considered by many the finest military memoirs ever written. Includes letters, historic photographs, maps and more. 528pp. 6⅛ x 9¼. 0-486-28587-1

ANCIENT EGYPTIAN MATERIALS AND INDUSTRIES, A. Lucas and J. Harris. Fascinating, comprehensive, thoroughly documented text describes this ancient civilization's vast resources and the processes that incorporated them in daily life, including the use of animal products, building materials, cosmetics, perfumes and incense, fibers, glazed ware, glass and its manufacture, materials used in the mummification process, and much more. 544pp. 6⅛ x 9¼. (Available in U.S. only.) 0-486-40446-3

RUSSIAN STORIES/RUSSKIE RASSKAZY: A Dual-Language Book, edited by Gleb Struve. Twelve tales by such masters as Chekhov, Tolstoy, Dostoevsky, Pushkin, others. Excellent word-for-word English translations on facing pages, plus teaching and study aids, Russian/English vocabulary, biographical/critical introductions, more. 416pp. 5⅜ x 8½. 0-486-26244-8

PHILADELPHIA THEN AND NOW: 60 Sites Photographed in the Past and Present, Kenneth Finkel and Susan Oyama. Rare photographs of City Hall, Logan Square, Independence Hall, Betsy Ross House, other landmarks juxtaposed with contemporary views. Captures changing face of historic city. Introduction. Captions. 128pp. 8¼ x 11. 0-486-25790-8

NORTH AMERICAN INDIAN LIFE: Customs and Traditions of 23 Tribes, Elsie Clews Parsons (ed.). 27 fictionalized essays by noted anthropologists examine religion, customs, government, additional facets of life among the Winnebago, Crow, Zuni, Eskimo, other tribes. 480pp. 6⅛ x 9¼. 0-486-27377-6

TECHNICAL MANUAL AND DICTIONARY OF CLASSICAL BALLET, Gail Grant. Defines, explains, comments on steps, movements, poses and concepts. 15-page pictorial section. Basic book for student, viewer. 127pp. 5⅜ x 8½. 0-486-21843-0

THE MALE AND FEMALE FIGURE IN MOTION: 60 Classic Photographic Sequences, Eadweard Muybridge. 60 true-action photographs of men and women walking, running, climbing, bending, turning, etc., reproduced from rare 19th-century masterpiece. vi + 121pp. 9 x 12. 0-486-24745-7

LIGHT AND SHADE: A Classic Approach to Three-Dimensional Drawing, Mrs. Mary P. Merrifield. Handy reference clearly demonstrates principles of light and shade by revealing effects of common daylight, sunshine, and candle or artificial light on geometrical solids. 13 plates. 64pp. 5⅜ x 8½. 0-486-44143-1

ASTROLOGY AND ASTRONOMY: A Pictorial Archive of Signs and Symbols, Ernst and Johanna Lehner. Treasure trove of stories, lore, and myth, accompanied by more than 300 rare illustrations of planets, the Milky Way, signs of the zodiac, comets, meteors, and other astronomical phenomena. 192pp. 8⅜ x 11. 0-486-43981-X

JEWELRY MAKING: Techniques for Metal, Tim McCreight. Easy-to-follow instructions and carefully executed illustrations describe tools and techniques, use of gems and enamels, wire inlay, casting, and other topics. 72 line illustrations and diagrams. 176pp. 8¼ x 10⅞. 0-486-44043-5

MAKING BIRDHOUSES: Easy and Advanced Projects, Gladstone Califf. Easy-to-follow instructions include diagrams for everything from a one-room house for bluebirds to a forty-two-room structure for purple martins. 56 plates; 4 figures. 80pp. 8¾ x 6⅜. 0-486-44183-0

LITTLE BOOK OF LOG CABINS: How to Build and Furnish Them, William S. Wicks. Handy how-to manual, with instructions and illustrations for building cabins in the Adirondack style, fireplaces, stairways, furniture, beamed ceilings, and more. 102 line drawings. 96pp. 8¾ x 6⅜. 0-486-44259-4

THE SEASONS OF AMERICA PAST, Eric Sloane. From "sugaring time" and strawberry picking to Indian summer and fall harvest, a whole year's activities described in charming prose and enhanced with 79 of the author's own illustrations. 160pp. 8¼ x 11. 0-486-44220-9

THE METROPOLIS OF TOMORROW, Hugh Ferriss. Generous, prophetic vision of the metropolis of the future, as perceived in 1929. Powerful illustrations of towering structures, wide avenues, and rooftop parks–all features in many of today's modern cities. 59 illustrations. 144pp. 8¼ x 11. 0-486-43727-2

THE PATH TO ROME, Hilaire Belloc. This 1902 memoir abounds in lively vignettes from a vanished time, recounting a pilgrimage on foot across the Alps and Apennines in order to "see all Europe which the Christian Faith has saved." 77 of the author's original line drawings complement his sparkling prose. 272pp. 5⅜ x 8½. 0-486-44001-X

THE HISTORY OF RASSELAS: Prince of Abissinia, Samuel Johnson. Distinguished English writer attacks eighteenth-century optimism and man's unrealistic estimates of what life has to offer. 112pp. 5⅜ x 8½. 0-486-44094-X

A VOYAGE TO ARCTURUS, David Lindsay. A brilliant flight of pure fancy, where wild creatures crowd the fantastic landscape and demented torturers dominate victims with their bizarre mental powers. 272pp. 5⅜ x 8½. 0-486-44198-9

Paperbound unless otherwise indicated. Available at your book dealer, online at **www.doverpublications.com**, or by writing to Dept. GI, Dover Publications, Inc., 31 East 2nd Street, Mineola, NY 11501. For current price information or for free catalogs (please indicate field of interest), write to Dover Publications or log on to **www.doverpublications.com** and see every Dover book in print. Dover publishes more than 500 books each year on science, elementary and advanced mathematics, biology, music, art, literary history, social sciences, and other areas.